▲▲▲

CHRISTMAS STOCKINGS IN CROSS-STITCH

by
Kooler Design Studio

▲▲▲

CHRISTMAS STOCKINGS IN CROSS-STITCH

KOOLER DESIGN STUDIO
President: Donna Kooler
Cross-Stitch Designers:
Linda Gillum, Nancy Rossi,
Barbara Baatz, Jorja Hernandez

CROSS STITCH & COUNTRY CRAFTS® MAGAZINE
Editors: Deanna West,
Kit Schlich, Paula Morgan
Contributing Editor: Todd Stone
Graphic Design: Marsha Jarvis
Contributing Designer: Deb van der Geugten
Special thanks to Kristina Chi, Lily Giang, Ina Klickstein,
Bill Konzak, Joanne Krueger, Ginny Lindsay, Gail Marell,
Robin Rogers, Sally Shimizu, and Carol Tolbert

CRAFTWAYS CORPORATION
Publisher: Dale Schenkelberg
Editor: Joan Cravens
Art Director: Jo Lynn Taylor

Features Editor: Deanna West
Stitchery Coordinator: Shirley Wilson
Project Assistants: Nita Balas, Theresa Ellerbusch, Sandra Hibbert

Text Editor: Kit Schlich
Assistant Text Editor: Paula Morgan
Staff Writer: Barbara Konzak-Kuhn
Editorial Coordinator: Florence Stone

Assistant Art Directors: Marsha Jarvis, Nancy Wong
Senior Cross-Stitch Designers: Sandy Orton, Donna Yuen
Cross-Stitch Designer: Pamela Johnson
Technical Illustrator: Micaela Carr

BETTER HOMES AND GARDENS® MAGAZINE
President, Better Homes and Gardens Magazine Group: William T. Kerr
Vice President/Publishing Director, Craftways: Jerry Ward

MEREDITH CORPORATION OFFICERS
Chairman of the Executive Committee: E. T. Meredith III
Chairman of the Board, President, and Chief Executive Officer: Jack D. Rehm

MERRY CHRISTMAS

Christmas stockings hold more than gifts. Every stocking is full of countless special memories, too. And each year when you hang your stockings in eager anticipation of the holidays, you have a chance to relive the special joys of Christmases past. The stocking designs in this book, created by the Kooler Design Studio designers, capture a variety of unique Christmas moments. Projects, by the editors of *Cross Stitch & Country Crafts*® magazine, help make each design special. Because of their ageless appeal and the time and love that you put into stitching them for yourself, family members, or friends, each stocking surely will become a meaningful memento, a source of excitement and joy for years to come.

CONTENTS

▲▲▲

SANTA'S
WORKSHOP

Designed by Linda Gillum

Christmas is drawing near.

And Santa is hard at work finishing

his toys before Christmas Eve. He's

got a lot to do, but with the help of

his elves the magical workshop comes to

life. Just as Santa puts his whole heart into

every toy he makes, you can put your love

into stitching a stocking, ornaments, gift

tags (right), and a pendant (above). This

fun design shows not only the joy of

giving—but the caring that

goes into creating a gift.

name

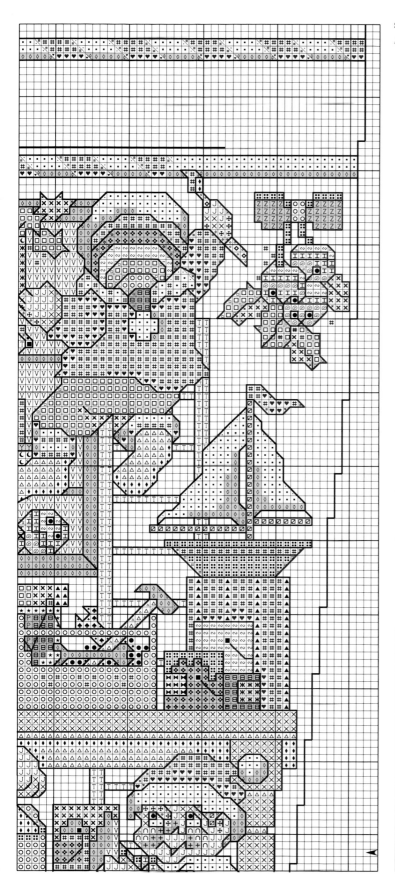

SANTA'S WORKSHOP ★ ★ ★ ★

Anchor		DMC	
002	· ·	000	white
110	I I	208	lavender - vy dk
105	★ ★	209	lavender - dk
403	■ ■	310	black
399	◆ ◆	318	pearl gray - med
347	△ △	402	mahogany - lt
020	♥ ♥	498	christmas red - dk
046	# #	666	christmas red - bright
923	▲ ▲	699	christmas green - vy dk
239	✕ ✕	702	kelly green
256	☐ ☐	704	chartreuse - bright
306	I I	725	topaz - med
942	T T	738	tan - vy lt
303	✳ ✳	742	tangerine - lt
301	∼ ∼	744	yellow - lt
868	✚ ✚	758	terra cotta - lt
397	◇ ◇	762	pearl gray - vy lt
024	∩ ∩	776	pink - med
307	⊚ ⊚	783	christmas gold
131	⦂⦂ ⦂⦂	798	delft blue - dk
130	○ ○	799	delft blue - med
128	Z Z	800	delft blue - lt
048	✛ ✛	818	baby pink
380	● ●	839	beige brown - dk
379	◊ ◊	840	beige brown - med
378	Λ Λ	841	beige brown - lt
376	B B	842	beige brown - vy lt
027	⌧ ⌧	899	rose - med
349	⊘ ⊘	921	copper - med
324	◆ ◆	922	copper - lt
920	V V	932	antique blue - med lt

347	✕ ✕	945	pink beige
330	⋈ ⋈	947	burnt orange - med
778	J J	948	peach flesh - vy lt
187	C C	958	aqua - dk
186	✺ ✺	959	aqua - med
185	Y Y	964	aqua - lt
316	◈ ◈	970	pumpkin - med
086	⊟ ⊟	3608	fuchsia - med
085	P P	3609	fuchsia - lt

Half cross (stitch in direction of symbol):

347	╱ ╱	402	mahogany - lt

Backstitch:

020		498	stripes on angel's dress, doll's mouth
400		317	personalization border, angel's wings, white parts of elves' clothes, panda's head, nose & tummy, sails of boat, Santa's hair, eyebrows, mustache, beard & shirt; doll's blouse & bow, tissue paper in box with bear
400		317	Santa's glasses, pail handles (2X)
132		797	outline of personalization (2X)
936		632	floor boards
380		838	heart string, eyes of bear & doll, nails (2X)
380		838	all other backstitching

Straight stitch:

380	╱	838	drum bindings, boot laces

Running stitch:

132		797	stitch lines in personalization (2X)
132		797	stitch lines on Santa's apron
			stocking outline

Stitch count: 221 high x 140 wide.
Fabrics and finished design sizes:

11 Aida, 20-1/8"h x 12-3/4"w
14 Aida, 15-7/8"h x 10"w
18 Aida, 12-3/8"h x 7-7/8"w
22 Hardanger, 10-1/8"h x 6-3/8"w

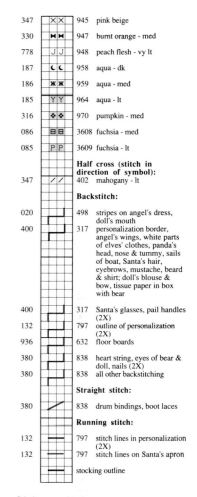

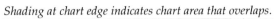

Shading at chart edge indicates chart area that overlaps.

motif A

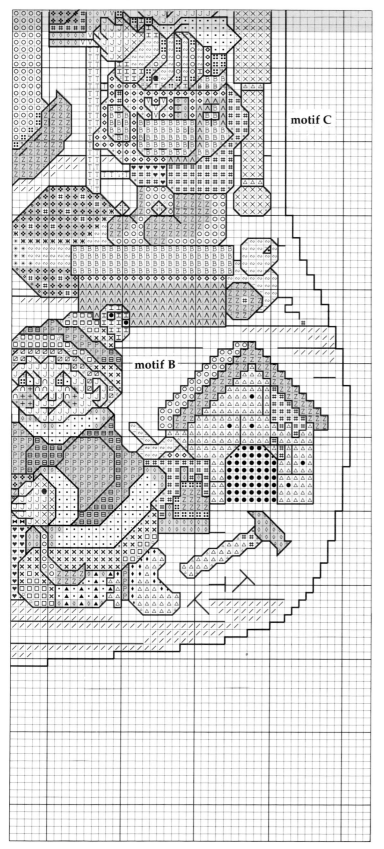

motif C

motif B

STOCKING

MATERIALS

- 15"x20" Ivory Jubilee (28-ct.)
- Floss listed in chart key; additional floss skeins needed— white(1), 402(1), 666(1), 762(1), 799(1), 838(1)
- ½ yd. ivory moiré faille
- ½ yd. cream cotton fabric
- ⅜ yd. red and white striped fabric
- 1⅛ yds. of ³⁄₁₆"-dia. cotton cord
- Sewing thread

INSTRUCTIONS

USE ½" SEAM ALLOWANCE.

1. Using 3 strands of floss for cross-stitch, center and stitch *Santa's Workshop* over 2 threads on Jubilee. Center and stitch name on baseline.

2. Sew running stitches around outer edge of design (see chart), allowing an extra ⅛" beyond design at top edge. Trim fabric ½" beyond running stitches.

3. Using design fabric as pattern, cut one stocking back from faille and 2 lining pieces from cotton fabric.

4. Cut and piece striped fabric into 2"x40" and 1½"x5" bias strips. Using longer strip and cord, make

piping; trim seam allowance to ½".

5. With raw edges even, baste piping to right side of design fabric along sides and foot.

6. With right sides together, sew stocking back to design unit; leave top open. Clip curves and turn right side out.

7. For hanger, fold shorter strip in half lengthwise; sew long edge. Trim seam to ¼", turn, and press.

8. Fold hanger in half; sew to right side of stocking back adjacent to piping (with raw edges even).

9. Sew lining pieces together along sides and foot, leaving 5" opening in one side. Trim seam allowance to ¼"; clip curves.

10. Insert stocking unit into lining, right sides facing; sew together around top edge. Trim seam and turn. Slip-stitch opening in lining closed.♣

PENDANT

MATERIALS

- 3½"x4" Cream Edinborough linen (36-ct.)
- Floss for motif (see key)
- Gold-tone pendant with 1½"x1⅞" design area
- Needlework Finisher

Continued on next page

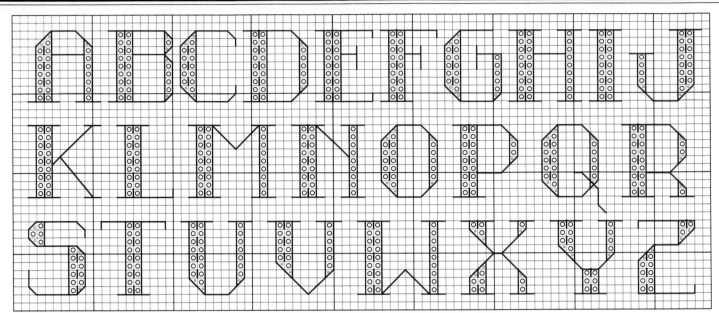

INSTRUCTIONS

1. Using 2 strands of floss for cross-stitch, center and stitch bow-with-bells and-holly motif from *Santa's Workshop* over 2 threads on linen.

2. Using transparent cover included with pendant, center and lightly trace outline onto back of design fabric. Cut fabric along line.

3. Apply Needlework Finisher sparingly to cut edge; let dry.

4. Assemble pendant, following manufacturer's instructions, omitting transparent cover.▲

ORNAMENT

MATERIALS FOR ONE

- 7"-sq. Cream Edinborough linen (36-ct.)
- Floss for motif (see key)

- 7"-sq. **each** polyester fleece, red fabric, heavy and lightweight cardboard
- ¼ yd. **each** green fabric and red and white striped fabric
- ½ yd. **each** ¹⁄₁₆"-dia. and ³⁄₁₆"-dia. cotton cord
- ¼ yd. of ¼"-W red grosgrain ribbon
- 4" of ⅛"-W red gros-grain ribbon
- 9mm gold-tone jingle bell
- Tacky glue
- Tracing paper
- Sewing thread

INSTRUCTIONS

1. Using 2 strands of floss for cross-stitch, center and stitch Motif A, B, **or** C from *Santa's Workshop* over 2 threads on linen.

2. Trace pattern for appropriate motif; cut out. Trace pattern onto backs of design fabric (design centered), red fabric

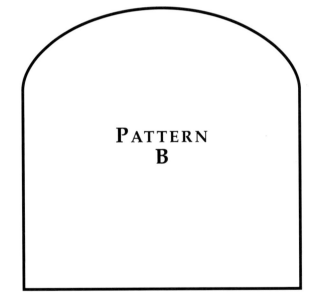

PATTERN B

(backing), polyester fleece, and cardboards. Cut fabrics 1" beyond traced line. Cut fleece and cardboards along line.

3. Glue fleece to heavy cardboard. Center fleece over back of design fabric; pull fabric edges to back of cardboard and glue.

4. Measure circumference of design unit. Cut and piece green fabric and striped fabric to make 1½"-W bias strips 1" longer than

circumference of design unit. Cut cords same length as strip. Using ¹⁄₁₆"-dia. cord and green strip, make piping. Using ³⁄₁₆"-dia. cord and striped strip, make piping; trim seam allowances to ½".

5. Glue green piping around outer edge of design unit, overlapping ends at center bottom. Repeat with striped piping.

6. Fold ⅛"-W ribbon in half. Glue raw ends to back

GIFT TAG PATTERN

PATTERN C

PATTERN A

of design unit at center top edge.

7. Round off bottom corners of lightweight cardboard to match curve of design unit. Center lightweight cardboard over wrong side of backing; pull fabric edges to back of cardboard and glue.

8. Glue wrong sides of design and backing units together.

9. Tie ¼"-W ribbon into a 2"-W bow; notch ribbon ends. Glue bow to front of design unit at center bottom edge. Tack bell to center of bow.♠

GIFT TAG

MATERIALS FOR ONE

• 7⅝"x5⅝" Ivory Aida 14
• Floss for motif (see key)
• 7⅝"x5⅝" ivory fabric with green and red Christmas print

• ¼ yd. red and white striped fabric
• 7⅝"x5⅝" fusible web
• 1 skein DMC #498 pearl cotton #5
• Tracing paper
• Sewing thread

INSTRUCTIONS

1. Trace gift tag pattern; cut out. Center pattern over back of Aida; trace lightly. Sew running stitches around traced lines.

2. Use 3 strands of floss for cross-stitch and use *Gift Tag* Alphabet (p. 9) for all lettering. For panda tag, stitch panda motif from *Santa's Workshop,* with left edge of motif 1⅛" from pointed side of outline and centered top to bottom. Stitch names to right of panda.

For angels tag, stitch angel motif from *Santa's Workshop,* with right edge ⅜" from short side of

outline and ½" above bottom edge. Repeat motif 4 squares to the left. Stitch names above angels.

For holly tag, stitch holly garland from top of *Santa's Workshop,* with right edge ⅜" from short side of outline and ⅜" below top edge. Stitch names below holly.

3. Using fusible web, fuse print fabric to back of design fabric, following manufacturer's instructions. Cut design unit

along running-stitch lines.

4. Cut 1"x13" bias strip from striped fabric. Press one long edge of strip under ¼". With raw edges matching and using ¼" seam allowance, sew long, unpressed edge of strip around edge of design unit, overlapping ends at point. Fold pressed edge of strip to back and slip-stitch.

5. Cut 8" length of pearl cotton. Thread pearl cotton through design unit ⅜" from point; knot ends.♠

HOLIDAY TOY SHELF

Designed by Nancy Rossi

At no other time in your life does Christmas

hold the same enchantment as when you are a child. It begins

with the expectation of Santa Claus coming

down your chimney and builds with the sheer excitement

of waking up to a Christmas tree surrounded by gifts. You

can share with other children that exciting time in your life

by stitching this lovely stocking and ornament.

You might just find that you get caught up in the child-like

excitement of Christmas all over again.

K eep all of your child's Christmas greetings in

this adorable card holder. It's a perfect decoration

for any youngster's room.

STOCKING

MATERIALS

- 19½"x7½" Red Aida 14
- Floss listed in chart key
- ½ yd. **each** red faille and red cotton fabric
- ¼ yd. green/red/blue plaid taffeta
- ⅛ yd. green taffeta
- 1¼ yds. of 3⁄16"-dia. cotton cord
- Sewing thread
- Dressmaker's chalk
- Graph paper
- Tracing paper

INSTRUCTIONS

USE ½" SEAM ALLOWANCE, UNLESS OTHERWISE NOTED.

1. Using 3 strands of floss for cross-stitch and referring to Fig. 1, stitch *Holiday Toy Shelf* on Aida, centering name on baseline. Trim 1" from all sides of design fabric. Using design fabric as pattern, cut red cotton fabric (backing).

2. With right sides facing, sew short edges of design fabric together; trim seam and turn.

3. With right sides facing, sew short edges of backing together; trim seams.

4. Cut and piece 3"x52" strip from plaid taffeta. Fold strip in half lengthwise, wrong sides facing; press. Beginning at one end and using dressmaker's chalk, make ¼"-L marks ½" apart along raw edges. Using marks as guides, hand-baste the strip into box pleats (Fig. 2).

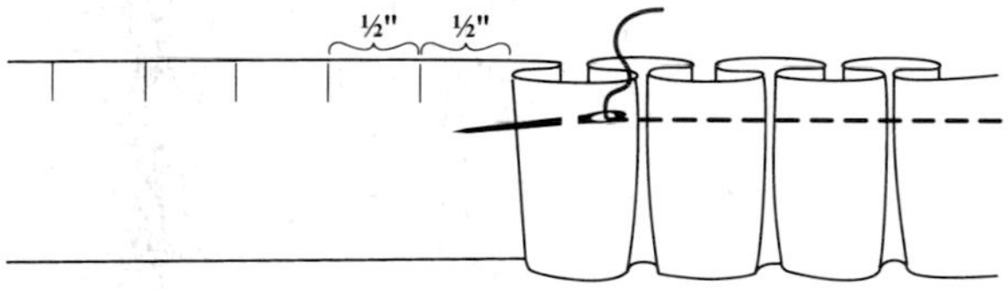

Figure 2

5. With raw edges matching, baste pleated strip to bottom edge of design fabric, overlapping ends at back and turning top end under ½".

6. With right sides facing, sew design unit and backing together along bottom edge; trim seam and turn.

7. Using graph paper, enlarge Stocking Pattern B (p. 106); cut 2 each from red faille and red cotton fabric. Trace heel and toe patterns (p. 21); cut one each from plaid taffeta.

8. Cut 1"x6½" (A) and 1"x6" (B) bias strips from green taffeta. With right sides facing and using ¼" seam allowance, sew A strip to inside edge of heel piece; press strip away from heel. Fold strip to back of heel; press. Repeat with B strip and toe piece.

9. With right side up, baste heel and toe pieces to top of one faille piece (stocking front; with toe pointing left) along raw edges. Sew heel and toe pieces to stocking front along bias-strip seams (Fig. 3).

10. Cut and piece 2"x40" bias strip from faille. Using strip and cord, make piping; trim seam allowance to ½".

11. With raw edges even and beginning 2" below top edge, baste piping to right side of stocking front, along sides and foot,

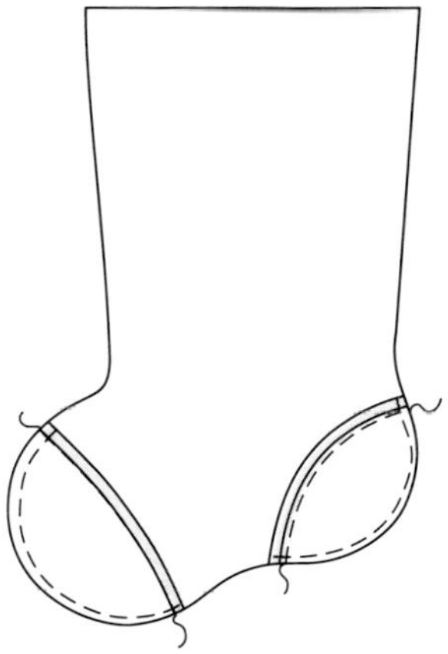

Figure 3

ending approximately 2" from top edge (Fig. 4).

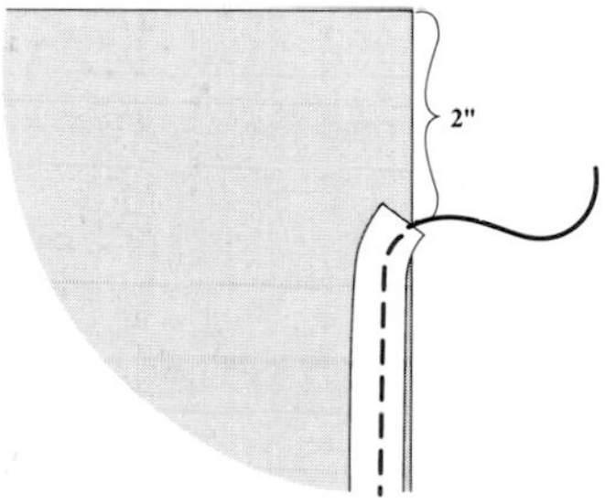

Figure 4

12. With right sides facing, sew stocking front and remaining faille piece together along sides and foot. Clip curves and turn right side out.

13. Sew red cotton (lining) pieces together along sides and foot; leave 5" opening along one side. Trim seam allowance; clip curves.

14. For hanger, cut 1½"x5" bias strip from faille. Fold strip in half lengthwise; sew long edge. Trim seam to ¼", turn, and press.

Continued on next page

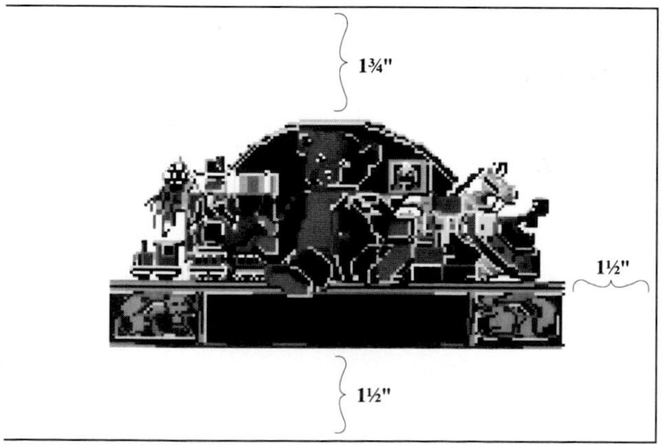

Figure 1

15. Fold hanger in half; sew to right side of lining back adjacent to back seam (with raw edges even).

16. With wrong side of cuff facing right side of faille and aligning seam of cuff with back seam of stocking unit, baste cuff to stocking unit around top edge.

17. Insert cuff unit into lining, right sides facing; sew together around top edge. Trim seam and turn. Slip-stitch opening in lining closed.▲

LARGE ORNAMENT

MATERIALS

- 7"-sq. Red Aida 14
- Floss for motif (see key)
- 5"-sq. **each** red fabric and lightweight cardboard
- ⅛ yd. green/red/blue plaid taffeta
- 14" of ⅛"-dia. metallic gold twisted cord
- 4"-dia. round Stik'N Puff
- 4" of ¼"-W red grosgrain ribbon
- Tacky glue
- Sewing thread

INSTRUCTIONS

1. Using 3 strands of floss for cross-stitch, center and stitch teddy bear motif from *Holiday Toy Shelf* on Aida.

2. Trace Stik'N Puff shape onto back of design fabric (design centered), red fabric (backing), and cardboard. Trim fabrics 1" beyond traced line. Cut cardboard along line.

3. Center foam side of Stik'N Puff over back of design fabric; remove backing paper. Press Stik'N Puff firmly against fabric. Pull fabric edges onto adhesive backing. Use glue where edges overlap.

4. Glue cord around edge of design unit; overlap ends at center top.

5. See Step 4 for Stocking, cutting 2½"x39" strip of plaid taffeta.

6. Glue pleated edge of strip around back edge of design unit, overlapping ends at top and folding top end under ½".

7. Fold ribbon in half. Glue raw edges to center top back of design unit.

8. Center cardboard over backing fabric; pull edges to back and glue. Glue wrong sides of design and backing units together.▲

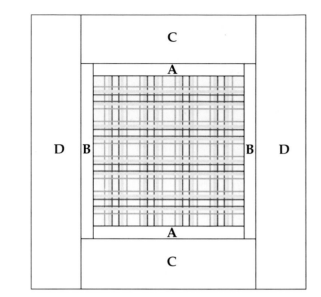

Figure 5

SMALL ORNAMENT

MATERIALS

- 4"-sq. Red Aida 14
- Floss for motif (see key)
- 4"-sq. **each** red fabric and lightweight cardboard
- ⅛ yd. green/red/blue plaid taffeta
- 9" of ⅛"-dia. metallic gold twisted cord
- 2¼"-dia. round Stik'N Puff
- 4" of ¼"-W red grosgrain ribbon
- Tacky glue
- Sewing thread

INSTRUCTIONS

1. Using 3 strands of floss for cross-stitch, center and stitch top motif from *Holiday Toy Shelf* on Aida.

2. See Steps 2–8 for Large Ornament, cutting 2½"x27" strip of plaid taffeta.▲

PEGGED FRAMED PIECE

MATERIALS

- 12"x8" Red Aida 14
- Floss listed in chart key
- Pegged dome frame with 9"x5" design area
- 11"x7" **each** polyester fleece, heavy and medium-weight cardboard
- Glazier points
- Sawtooth frame hanger
- Tacky glue

INSTRUCTIONS

1. Using 3 strands of floss for cross-stitch, center and stitch *Holiday Toy Shelf* on Aida, centering "Cards" on baseline.

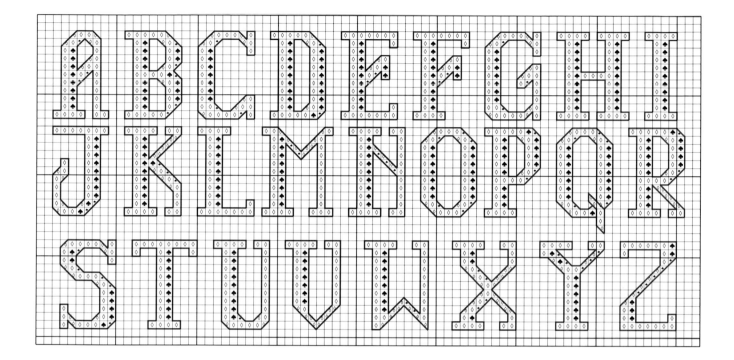

2. Trace inside back edge of frame onto heavy cardboard; cut out. Using heavy cardboard as pattern, cut fleece and remaining cardboard. Glue fleece to heavy cardboard.

3. Place fleece unit atop back of design fabric with bottom edge ½" below bottom edge of design; center side to side. Trace around cardboard lightly; cut design fabric 1" beyond traced line.

4. Center design fabric right side up atop fleece unit; pull edges to back and glue.

5. Insert design unit into frame, followed by remaining cardboard; secure with glazier points. Attach frame hanger to center top back edge of frame.▲

CARD HOLDER POCKET

MATERIALS

- ⅛ yd. green taffeta
- ¼ yd. green/red/blue plaid taffeta
- ⅜ yd. **each** red cotton and red faille fabric
- ¾ yd. of ¼"-W red grosgrain ribbon
- 1 yd. of 1"-W blue grosgrain ribbon

INSTRUCTIONS

USE ½" SEAM ALLOWANCE.

1. Cut 7"-sq. plaid taffeta. Cut green taffeta into two 1½"x7" (A) and two 1½"x8" (B) strips. Cut red faille into two 2½"x8" (C) and two 2½"x11" (D) strips. Referring to Fig. 5, sew strips to plaid taffeta in alphabetical order, with right sides facing; press each strip away from plaid taffeta as you proceed.

2. Cut one 11"-sq. piece of red faille (backing) and one 11"x20" piece of red cotton (lining).

3. With right sides facing, sew backing to plaid unit along sides and bottom; trim seams, clip corners, and turn.

4. Fold lining in half, right sides facing and matching short (top) edges. Sew sides of lining, leaving 5" opening in one side; clip corners. Press seams open.

5. Cut four 6" lengths of red ribbon; fold each in half. Referring to Fig. 6, baste ribbons to right side of backing, matching raw edges.

Figure 6

6. Insert plaid unit into lining, with right sides facing; sew around top edge. Turn design unit right side out; slip-stitch opening in lining.

7. Tie blue ribbon into 3½"-W bow; notch ends. Tack bow to upper left corner of pocket front (see photo). Decoratively arrange and tack ends to pocket front.

8. Hang pocket from pegs of Framed Piece.▲

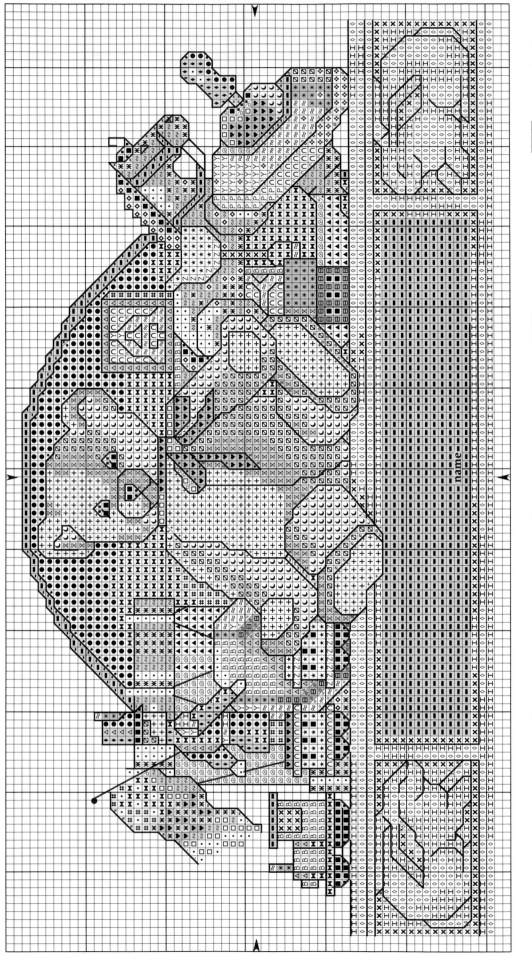

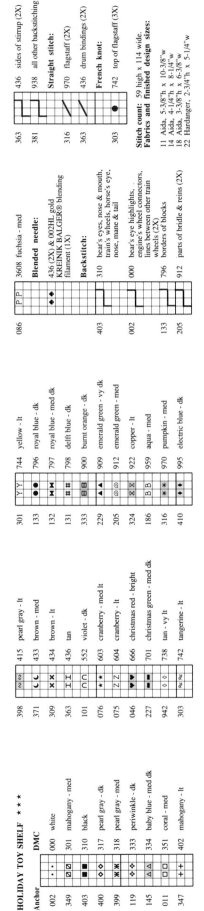

HOLIDAY TOY SHELF ★ ★ ★

Anchor			DMC	
002	·	·	000	white
349	▨	▨	301	mahogany - med
403	■	■	310	black
400	◇	◇	317	pearl gray - dk
399	✳	✳	318	pearl gray - med
119	❖	❖	333	periwinkle - dk
145	△	△	334	baby blue - med dk
011	□	□	351	coral - med
347	+	+	402	mahogany - lt

398	⌀	⌀	415	pearl gray - lt
371	☽	☽	433	brown - med
309	✕	✕	434	brown - lt
363	Ⅱ	Ⅱ	436	tan
101	⊂	⊂	552	violet - dk
076	★	★	603	cranberry - med lt
075	Z	Z	604	cranberry - lt
046	▶	▶	666	christmas red - bright
227	■	■	701	christmas green - med dk
942	◇	◇	738	tan - vy lt
303	≈	≈	742	tangerine - lt

301			744	yellow - lt
133	●	●	796	royal blue - lt
132	☒	☒	797	royal blue - med dk
131	#	#	798	delft blue - dk
333	⊟	⊟	900	burnt orange - dk
229	◀	◀	909	emerald green - vy dk
205	@	@	912	emerald green - med
324	⊠	⊠	922	copper - lt
186	B	B	959	aqua - med
316	✳	✳	970	pumpkin - med
410	◆	◆	995	electric blue - dk

| 086 | | | 3608 | fuchsia - med |

Blended needle:

| P | P | | 436 (2X) & 002HL gold KREINIK BALGER® blending filament (1X) |

Backstitch:

403		310	bear's eyes, nose & mouth, train's wheels, horse's eye, nose, mane & tail
002		000	bear's eye highlights, engine's wheel connectors, lines between other train wheels (2X)
133		796	borders of blocks
205		912	parts of bridle & reins (2X)
363		436	sides of stirrup (2X)
381		938	all other backstitching

Straight stitch:

| 316 | | 970 | flagstaff (2X) |
| 363 | | 436 | drum bindings (2X) |

French knot:

| 303 | ● | 742 | top of flagstaff (3X) |

Stitch count: 59 high x 114 wide.
Fabrics and finished design sizes:
11 Aida, 5-3/8"h x 10-3/8"w
14 Aida, 4-1/4"h x 8-1/4"w
18 Aida, 3-3/8"h x 6-3/8"w
22 Hardanger, 2-3/4"h x 5-1/4"w

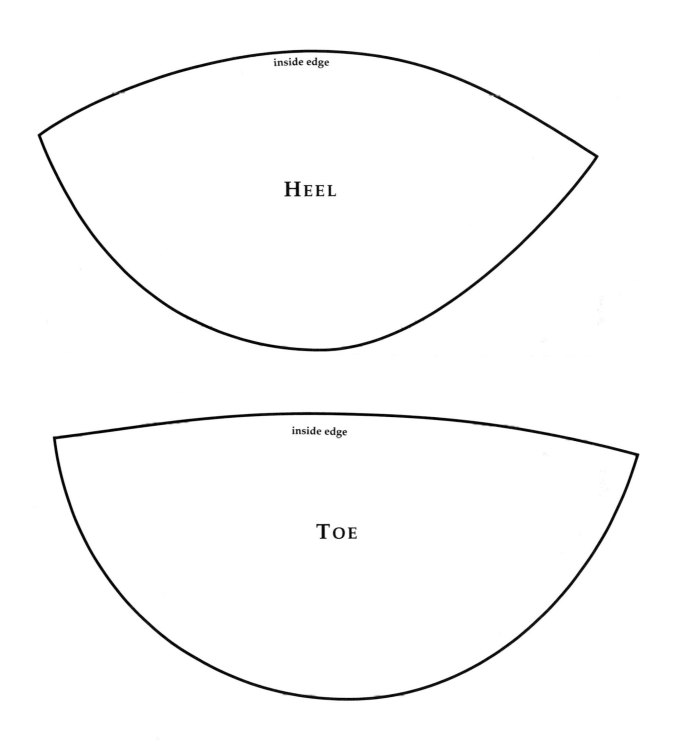

inside edge

HEEL

inside edge

TOE

HEEL AND TOE PATTERNS (FULL SIZE)

SNOWY FOREST EVENING

Designed by Nancy Rossi

The peacefulness of a winter evening.

If you listen carefully you can hear the rustle of deer,

deep in the forest, feasting on holly berries. A doe

and a buck pause undisturbed in a grove of frosted

evergreens. Savor this magical moment with a

magnificent stocking, ornament, and framed piece.

They will bring the beauty of nature to you and your

loved ones for generations to come.

name

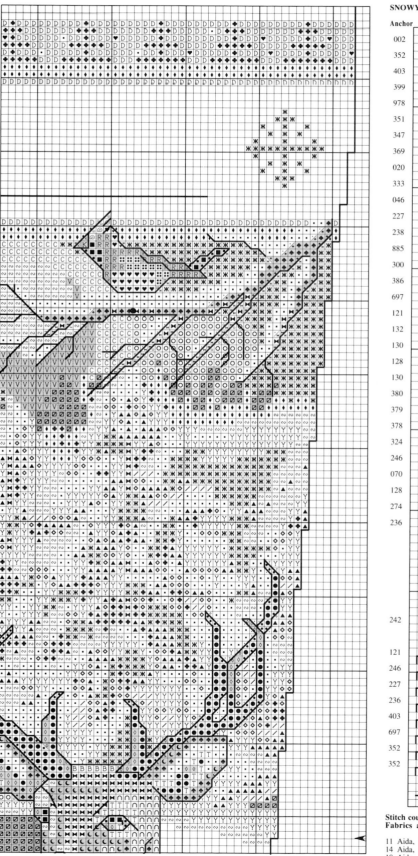

SNOWY FOREST EVENING ★ ★ ★

Anchor		DMC	
002	· ·	000	white
352	⋈ ⋈	300	mahogany - vy dk
403	■ ■	310	black
399	◊ ◊	318	pearl gray - med
978	◆ ◆	322	navy blue - vy lt
351	✛ ✛	400	mahogany - dk
347	K K	402	mahogany - lt
369	❖ ❖	435	brown - vy lt
020	♥ ♥	498	christmas red - dk
333	⊘ ⊘	608	orange - bright
046	R R	666	christmas red - bright
227	◇ ◇	701	christmas green - med dk
238	D D	703	chartreuse
885	J J	739	tan - ultra vy lt
300	V V	745	yellow - vy lt
386	∾ ∾	746	off white
697	T T	762	pearl gray - vy lt
121	★ ★	793	cornflower blue - med
132	✦ ✦	797	royal blue - med dk
130	⧄ ⧄	799	delft blue - med
128	O O	800	delft blue - lt
130	⋇ ⋇	809	delft blue - med lt
380	◆ ◆	838	beige brown - vy dk
379	C C	840	beige brown - med
378	∩ ∩	841	beige brown - lt
324	△ △	922	copper - lt
246	▲ ▲	986	forest green - vy dk
070	⦂⦂ ⦂⦂	3685	mauve - vy dk
128	Y Y	3753	antique blue - vy lt (1X)
274	C C	3756	baby blue - vy lt
236	● ●	3799	steel gray - vy dk

Blended needle:

	S S		211 (1X) & 800 (2X)
	I I		3041 (1X) & 932 (2X)
	B B		921 (1X) & 301 (2X)

Half cross:

242	/ /	989	forest green - med

Backstitch:

121		793	personalization (2X)
246		986	part of bushes (2X)
227		701	rest of bushes (2X)
236		3799	antlers
403		310	eyes & noses of deer, cardinals' tails & throat (2X)
697		762	highlights on eyes & noses of deer (2X)
352		300	part of branches (2X)
352		300	all other backstitching

Running stitch:

			Stocking outline

Stitch count: 222 high x 141 wide.
Fabrics and finished design sizes:

11 Aida, 20-1/4"h x 12-7/8"w
14 Aida, 15-7/8"h x 10-1/8"w
18 Aida, 12-3/8"h x 7-7/8"w
22 Hardanger, 10-1/8"h x 6-1/2"w

Shading at chart edge indicates chart area that overlaps.

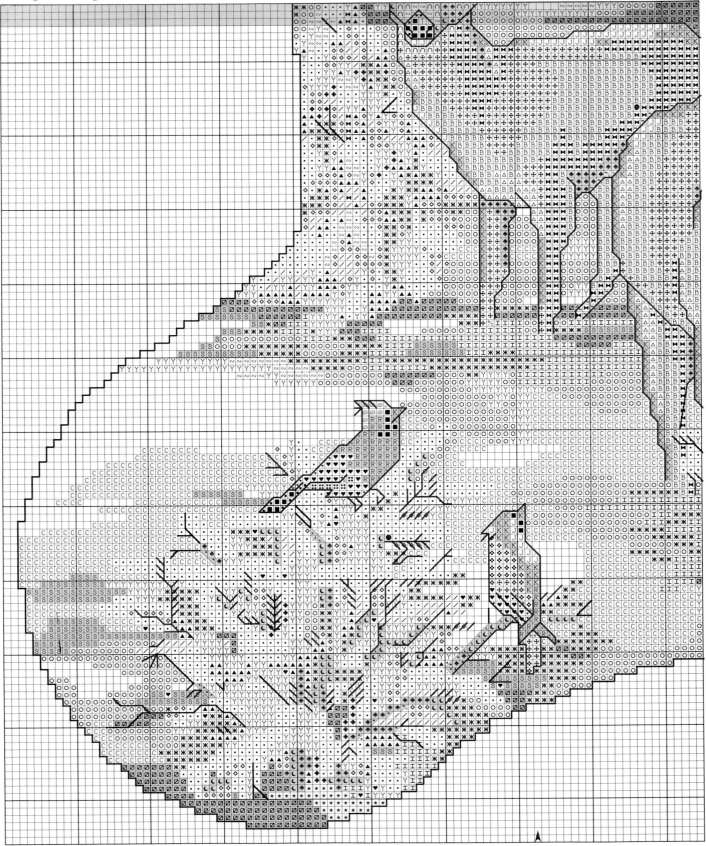

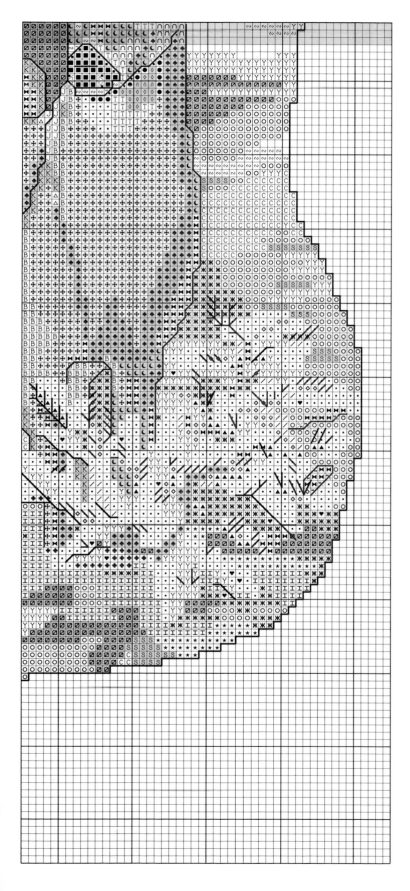

STOCKING

MATERIALS

- 15"x20" White Jobelan (28-ct.)
- Floss listed in chart key; additional floss skeins needed—white(2), 800(2), 809(2), 3753(1), 3756(1)
- 1 yd. green cotton fabric
- 1⅛ yds. of ³⁄₁₆"-dia. cotton cord
- Sewing thread

INSTRUCTIONS

USE ½" SEAM ALLOWANCE.

1. Center and stitch *Snowy Forest Evening* over 2 threads on Jobelan, using 3 strands of floss. Center and stitch name on baseline, omitting snowflakes as necessary.

2. Sew running stitches around outer edge of design (see chart), allowing an extra ⅛" beyond design at top edge. Trim fabric ½" beyond running stitches.

3. Using design fabric as pattern, cut one stocking back and 2 lining pieces from green fabric.

4. Cut and piece remaining green fabric into 2"x40" and 1¼"x5" bias strips. Using longer strip and cord, make piping; trim seam allowance to ½".

5. With raw edges even, baste piping to right side of design fabric along sides and foot.

6. With right sides facing, sew stocking back to design unit; leave top open. Clip curves and turn right side out.

7. For hanger, fold shorter strip in half lengthwise; sew long edge. Trim seam to ¼", turn, and press.

8. Fold hanger in half; sew to right side of stocking back adjacent to piping (with raw edges even).

9. Sew lining pieces together along sides and foot, leaving 5" opening in one side. Trim seam allowance to ¼"; clip curves.

10. Insert stocking unit into lining, right sides facing; sew together around top edge. Trim seam and turn. Slip-stitch opening in lining closed.▲

Continued on next page

ORNAMENT

MATERIALS FOR ONE

- 7"-sq. White Jobelan (28-ct.)
- Floss for motif (see key)
- 7"-sq. lightweight cardboard
- ¼ yd. green fabric
- 15" of 1"-W red premade pleated satin ruffle
- 15" of ³⁄₁₆"-dia. cotton cord
- 4"-dia. round Stik'N Puff
- 4" of ¼"-W red grosgrain ribbon
- Tacky glue
- Sewing thread

INSTRUCTIONS

1. Lightly trace Stik'N Puff onto back of Jobelan. Aligning blue dot on chart with center of traced area, stitch one cardinal motif from *Snowy Forest Evening* over 2 threads, using 3 strands of floss. Continue stitching 2 squares beyond traced line.

2. Trace Stik'N Puff onto back of green fabric (backing) and cardboard. Trim design fabric and green fabric 1" beyond traced line. Cut cardboard along line.

3. Center foam side of Stik'N Puff over back of design; remove backing paper. Press Stik'N Puff firmly against fabric. Pull fabric edges onto adhesive backing. Glue where edges overlap.

4. Center cardboard over backing fabric, pull edges to back, and glue.

5. Cut and piece remaining green fabric to make 2"x15" bias strip. Using strip and cord, make piping; trim seam allowance to ½".

6. Glue flat edge of piping around back edge of design unit, overlapping ends at top.

7. Glue pleated edge of ruffle around back edge of

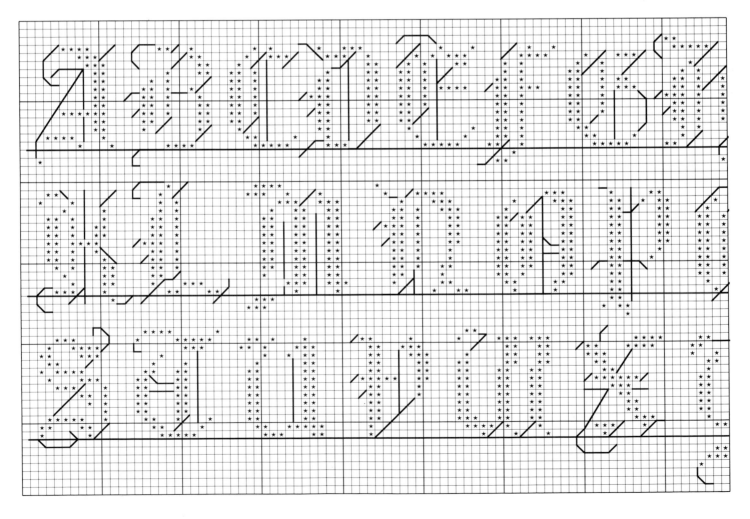

design unit, overlapping ends at top and turning top end under.

8. Fold ribbon in half. Glue raw ends to back edge of design unit at center top.

9. Glue design and backing units together.🌲

FRAMED PIECE

MATERIALS

- 9"x11" White Jobelan (28-ct.)

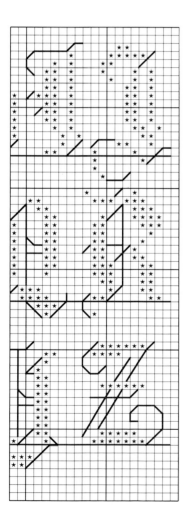

- Floss for motif (see key)
- 6⅛"x8⅛" honey-pine oval frame
- 7"x9" **each** polyester fleece, heavy and lightweight cardboard
- Glazier points
- Sawtooth frame hanger
- Light-colored sewing thread
- Tacky glue

INSTRUCTIONS

1. Lightly trace inner edge of frame onto back of Jobelan. Aligning blue dot on chart with center of traced area, stitch deer from *Snowy Forest Evening* over 2 threads using 3 strands of floss. Continue stitching 2 squares beyond traced line.

2. Trace back inside edge of frame onto lightweight cardboard; cut out. Using this as pattern, cut fleece and heavy cardboard.

3. Glue fleece to heavy cardboard.

4. Trim fabric 1" beyond design. Sew gathering thread ½" from raw edge. Center design right side up over fleece unit; draw up gathers on wrong side and secure thread. Glue fabric to back of cardboard.

5. Insert design unit and lightweight cardboard into frame; secure with glazier points.

6. Attach frame hanger to top center back edge of frame.🌲

Duplicate Stitch *For project on page 45.*

Before you begin stitching, rinse cotton floss: remove labels from floss skeins and thoroughly but carefully rinse floss (still wound) in cold water until bleeding stops. Add a small amount of vinegar to the last rinse water to set the dye. Let floss dry and replace labels.

If you select a washable sweater, wash it before stitching.

1. The stockinette stitch of the sweater is wider than it is high. A common duplicate stitch gauge is 6x8 (6 stitches per inch wide by 8 stitches per inch high). Proportions of a cross-stitch design will be altered.

2. Use six strands of floss for sweater gauges 6x8 and 7x9. For smaller gauges, you may want to experiment, stitching with 3–5 strands on a section of the sweater to find the coverage you want. Keep in mind that the sweater will show through your stitching;

this is part of the "look" of duplicate stitch.

3. Use a Size 18 tapestry needle for stitching. Begin stitching with a waste knot: tie a knot in one end of your floss, insert needle into front of sweater, approximately 3" from where you will begin stitching. For first duplicate stitch, bring needle up at the base of the "V" stitch on the sweater. Following knit of sweater, insert needle under base of stitch above (Fig. 1) and back down where

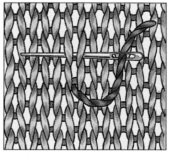

Fɪɢ. 1

stitch began (at base of "V"). Each "V" of the sweater knit corresponds to one square on the chart. Following chart, work

horizontally back and forth across fabric. It is acceptable to carry floss loosely on back 1"– 1½". To work vertically, work from top to bottom.

Allow 2"–2½" at end of floss length to tie off: weave floss under 3 stitches in one direction, then under 3 stitches in the other direction. To finish the waste knot, clip knot on front of sweater. Pull tail to underside of sweater and thread onto needle. Tie off floss as directed above. Begin new lengths of floss by weaving through back of previous stitching.

4. Use 3–4 strands of floss for backstitching. When making vertical backstitches, use light tension so the stitch doesn't "sink" into the ditch between the duplicate stitches. When backstitching horizontally, the lower part of the "V" from the stitch above may show below the backstitch. This occurs because of the overlapping nature of knit stitches and, again, is part of the "look" of duplicate stitch.

CHRISTMAS CARDINALS

Designed by Barbara Baatz

Not all birds fly south for the winter.

Some stay around for Christmas. Against a background of new

snow and holly branches, these colorful cardinals will add brilliance to any room.

The classic red stocking and ornament (right) will fit nicely in your

Christmas decorating scheme. And if you love birds and bright colors,

you can enjoy the pillow and framed piece, year 'round.

This beautiful Christmas Cardinals pillow

is sure to inject a warm, lively note into your

winter home. And the matching ornament will be

a beautiful addition to your Christmas tree.

STOCKING

MATERIALS

- 19½"x7½" Tea-dyed linen (28-ct.)
- Floss listed in chart key
- 17½"x5½" lightweight fusible interfacing
- ¼ yd. beige cotton fabric
- ¾ yd. dark red velvet
- ½ yd. red cotton fabric
- 1 yd. of ³⁄₁₆"-dia. cotton cord
- 1 yd. metallic gold and green piping
- Sewing thread
- Graph paper

INSTRUCTIONS

USE ½" SEAM ALLOWANCE.

1. Referring to Fig. 1, stitch *Christmas Cardinals* over 2 threads on linen, using 3 strands of floss for cross-stitch and centering name on baseline. Trim 1" from all sides of design fabric. Using design fabric as pattern, cut beige fabric (backing).

2. Fuse interfacing to back of design fabric, following manufacturer's instructions. With right sides facing, sew short edges of design unit together; trim seam and turn.

3. With right sides facing, sew short edges of backing together; trim seams.

4. Cut piping in half. With raw edges even, baste piping around right side of design unit along top and bottom edges, overlapping ends at seam.

5. With right sides facing, sew design unit and backing together along bottom edge; trim seam and turn.

6. Using graph paper, enlarge Stocking Pattern B (p. 106); cut 2 each of velvet and red cotton fabric.

7. Cut and piece remaining velvet into 2"x36" and 1½"x5" bias strips. Using longer strip and cotton cord, make piping; trim seam allowance to ½".

8. With raw edges even and beginning 2" below top edge, baste piping to right side of one velvet piece, along sides and foot, ending approx. 2" from top edge (Fig. 2).

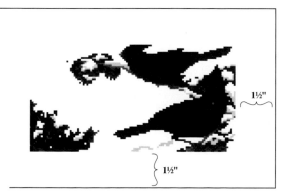

Figure 2

9. With right sides facing, sew velvet pieces together along sides and foot. Clip curves and turn right side out.

10. Sew cotton (lining) pieces together along sides and foot; leave 5" opening along one side. Trim seam allowance; clip curves.

11. For hanger, fold 5" bias strip in half lengthwise; sew long edge. Trim seam to ¼", turn, and press.

12. Fold hanger in half; sew to right side of lining back adjacent to back seam (with raw edges even).

13. With wrong side of cuff facing right side of velvet and aligning seam of cuff with back seam of stocking unit, baste cuff to stocking unit around top edge.

14. Insert cuff unit into lining, right sides facing; sew together around top edge. Trim seam and turn. Slip-stitch opening in lining closed.🌲

FRAMED PIECE

MATERIALS

- 15"x12" Tea-dyed linen (28-ct.)
- Floss listed in chart key
- 11⅜"x8¼" pecan-stained frame with gold accent
- Two mats, Chinese red with 8⅜"x5¼" opening and white with 8⅛"x5" opening

INSTRUCTIONS

1. Center and stitch *Christmas Cardinals* over 2 threads on linen, using 3 strands of floss for cross-stitch. Frame design.🌲

ORNAMENT

MATERIALS

- 6¾"-sq. Tea-dyed linen (28-ct.)
- Floss for motif (see key)
- 4¾"-sq. lightweight fusible interfacing
- 2¾"-sq. **each** heavy cardboard, polyester fleece, and red felt
- 5" of ¼"-W green satin ribbon
- 12½" of metallic gold and green piping
- Tacky glue

Continued on page 35

Figure 1

[cross-stitch chart of a cardinal with 1½" dimension markings]

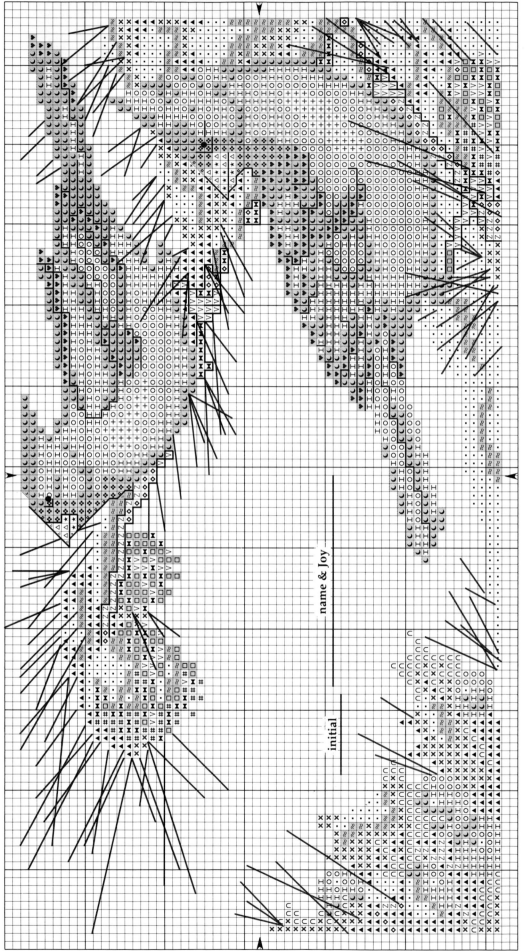
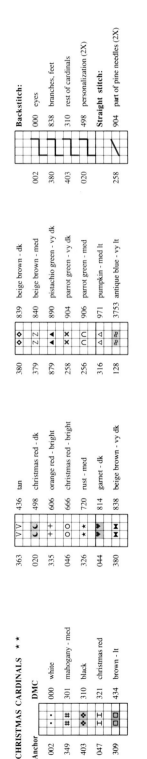

name & Joy

initial

French knot:

890	rest of pine needles (2X)	
000	eyes	

Stitch count: 60 high x 114 wide.
Fabrics and finished design sizes:
11 Aida, 5-1/2"h x 10-3/8"w
14 Aida, 4-3/8"h x 8-1/4"w
18 Aida, 3-3/8"h x 6-3/8"w
22 Hardanger, 2-3/4"h x 5-1/4"w

Backstitch:

000	eyes	002
838	branches, feet	380
310	rest of cardinals	403
498	personalization (2X)	020

Straight stitch:

904	part of pine needles (2X)	258

	Anchor	DMC	
◇	380	839	beige brown - dk
Z	379	840	beige brown - med
◀	879	890	pistachio green - vy dk
✕	258	904	parrot green - vy dk
∪	256	906	parrot green - med
△	316	971	pumpkin - med lt
≋	128	3753	antique blue - vy lt

	Anchor	DMC	
V	363	436	tan
∪	020	498	christmas red - dk
+	335	606	orange red - bright
O	046	666	christmas red - bright
★	326	720	rust - med
▶	044	814	garnet - dk
⊠	380	838	beige brown - vy vy dk

CHRISTMAS CARDINALS ★★

	Anchor	DMC	
·	002	000	white
#	349	301	mahogany - med
◆	403	310	black
H	047	321	christmas red
□	309	434	brown - lt

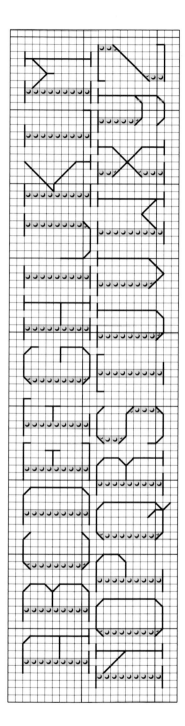

INSTRUCTIONS

1. Using 3 strands of floss for cross-stitch, stitch holly motif from lower left corner of *Christmas Cardinals* over 2 threads on linen with left and bottom edges 2" from edges of fabric. Stitch initial from *Snowy Forest Evening* Alphabet (pp. 28–29) on baseline, using DMC #815.

2. Trim 1" from all sides of design fabric. Fuse interfacing to design fabric following manufacturer's instructions.

3. Glue fleece to cardboard. Center fleece unit over back of design unit, aligning 2 edges with left and bottom edges of design; pull design fabric edges to back of cardboard and glue.

4. Beginning at center bottom, glue flat edge of piping around design unit, overlapping ends.

5. Fold ribbon in half. Glue ends to center top back edge of design unit.

6. Glue felt to back of design unit.▲

PILLOW

MATERIALS

- 11"x9" Tea-dyed linen (28-ct.)
- Floss listed in chart key
- ⅜ yd. red velvet
- 11"x9" lightweight fusible interfacing
- 35" of ³⁄₁₆"-dia. cotton cord
- Polyester fiberfill
- Sewing thread

INSTRUCTIONS

1. Using 3 strands of floss for cross-stitch, center and stitch *Christmas Cardinals* over 2 threads on linen; center "Joy" on baseline, using *Snowy Forest Evening* Alphabet (pp. 28–29) and DMC #815.

2. Fuse interfacing to back of design fabric, following manufacturer's instructions.

3. Trim design unit ½" beyond design at sides, ¾" beyond design at top, and 1" beyond design at bottom.

4. Using design unit as pattern, cut one velvet piece.

5. With right sides facing and using 1" seam allowance, sew velvet and design unit together along bottom edge of design. Fold velvet away from design unit.

6. Using pillow top as pattern, cut one velvet piece (backing).

7. Cut and piece remaining velvet into 2"x35" bias strip. Using strip and cord, make piping; trim seam allowance to ½".

8. With raw edges even, baste piping around right side of pillow top, overlapping ends at one side, even with seam.

9. With right sides facing and using ½" seam allowance, sew top and backing together; leave 4" opening on one side. Trim seams and turn.

10. Fill pillow firmly with fiberfill. Slip-stitch opening closed.▲

COLONIAL HERITAGE SAMPLER

Designed by Barbara Baatz

Christmas is a time to enjoy your favorite

traditions. Many families have customs and heirlooms that

they pass down through generations. And each year these

traditions seem to become more important. This Christmas might

be the time to include a traditional sampler in your

holiday decorating plans. Its classic alphabets and floral

motifs will help you create a stocking, basket band, lamp

trim (right), and a heart-shaped tree ornament (above)

that look like antique masterpieces.

This stocking and bellpull—in a new palette of

colors—just may become new family

heirlooms that will be treasured

for decades to come.

All the tradition and elegance of colonial

times are displayed in this unique wreath holder

and sweater. You can enjoy the wreath throughout

the Christmas season, while the sweater will

keep you cozy all winter long.

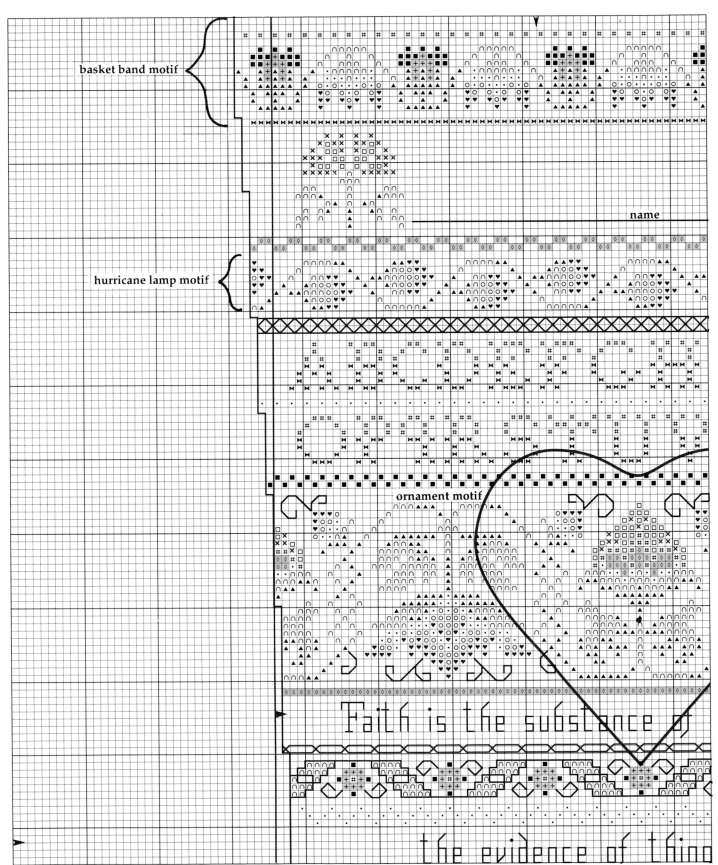

basket band motif

hurricane lamp motif

name

ornament motif

Faith is the substance of

the evidence of thing

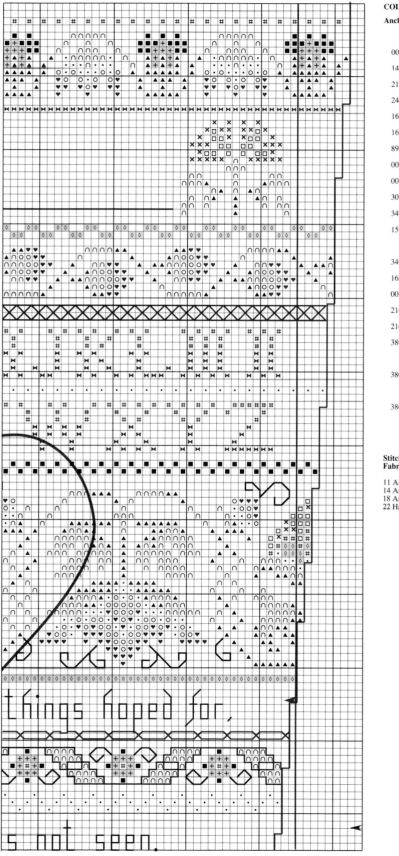

COLONIAL HERITAGE SAMPLER ★

Anchor		DMC	DMC color variation
		Pastel	Cranberry
002	· ·	white	white
145	■ ■	334	347
216	▲ ▲	367	469
240	∩ ∩	368	471
168	✕ ✕	597	816
167	▢ ▢	598	3328
891	◇ ◇	676	676
009	♥ ♥	760	3328
008	○ ○	761	760
307	# #	783	783
349	⋈ ⋈	921	921
159	+ +	3325	760

Backstitch:

349		921	921	row under 1st part of saying
168		597	816	row under 2nd part of saying (2X)
002		white	white	circles under 2nd part of saying
216		367	469	leaves
216		367	469	vines (2X)
380		838	890	all other backstitching

French knot:

| 380 | ● | 838 | 890 | saying |

Lazy daisy stitch:

| 380 | | 838 | 890 | flowers below lowercase alphabet |

Running stitch:

stocking outline

Stitch count: 220 high x 140 wide.
Fabrics and finished design sizes:

11 Aida, 20"h x 12-3/4"w
14 Aida, 15-3/4"h x 10"w
18 Aida, 12-1/4"h x 7-7/8"w
22 Hardanger, 10"h x 6-3/8"w

Shading at chart edge indicates chart area that overlaps.

the evidence of thing

Hebrews

sweater motif

wreath holder motif

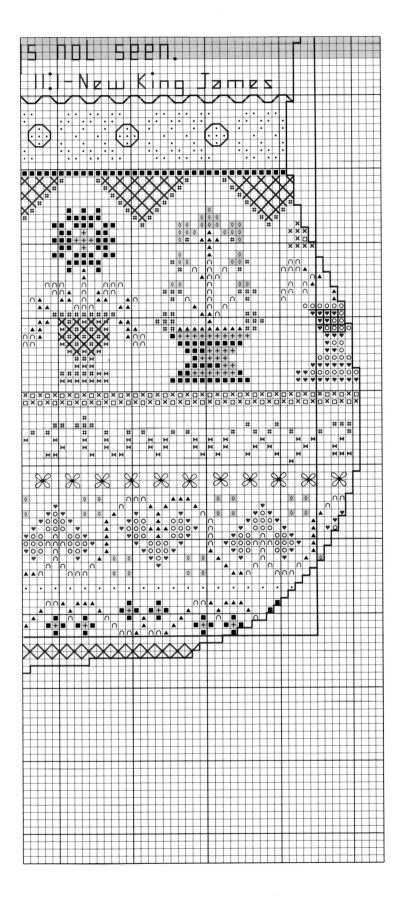

s not seen.
11:1-New King James

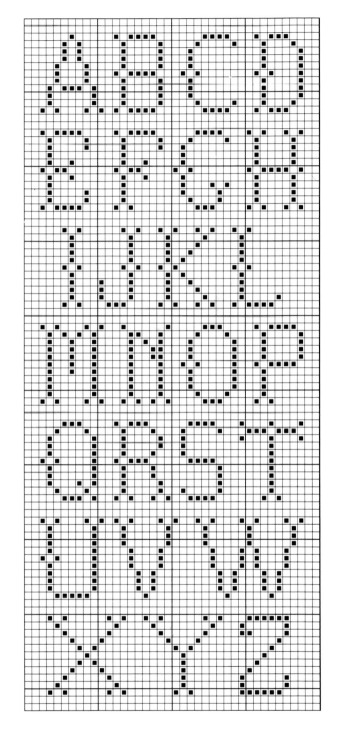

STOCKING

MATERIALS

- 15"x20" Natural linen (28-ct.)
- Floss listed in chart key; additional floss skeins needed—367(1), 368(1) for pastel variation; 469(1), 471(1) for cranberry variation
- 1 yd. fabric (green for pastel variation and red for cranberry variation)
- 15"x20" lightweight fusible interfacing
- 1⅛ yds. of ³⁄₁₆"-dia. cotton cord
- Sewing thread

INSTRUCTIONS

USE ½" SEAM ALLOWANCE.

1. Using 3 strands of floss for cross-stitch, center and stitch pastel or cranberry variation of *Colonial Heritage Sampler* over 2 threads on linen. Center and stitch name on baseline, omitting flowers as necessary.

2. Fuse interfacing to back of design fabric, following manufacturer's instructions.

3. Sew running stitches around outer edge of design (see chart), allowing an extra ¼" beyond design at top edge. Trim fabric ½" beyond running stitches.

4. Using design unit as pattern, cut one stocking back and 2 lining pieces from fabric.

5. Cut and piece remaining fabric into 2"x40" and 1½"x5" bias strips. Using longer strip and cord, make piping; trim seam to ½".

6. With raw edges even, baste piping to right side of design unit along sides and foot.

7. With right sides together, sew stocking back to design unit; leave top open. Clip curves and turn right side out.

8. For hanger, fold shorter strip in half lengthwise; sew long edge. Trim seam to ¼", turn, and press.

9. Fold hanger in half; sew to right side of stocking back adjacent to piping (with raw edges even).

10. Sew lining pieces together along sides and foot, leave 5" opening in one side. Trim seam allowance to ¼"; clip curves.

11. Insert stocking unit into lining, right sides facing; sew together around top edge. Trim seam and turn. Slip-stitch opening in lining closed.▲

BELLPULL

MATERIALS

- 11"x21½" Natural linen (28-ct.)
- Floss for motif (see key); additional floss skeins needed—367(1), 368(1)
- ⅜ yd. green fabric
- 11"x21½" lightweight fusible interfacing
- 21 cm-W brass bellpull hardware
- Sewing thread

INSTRUCTIONS

1. Referring to blue arrows for centering and blue lines for sides and bottom of design, center and stitch pastel variation of bellpull motif, extending bands as necessary; omit lowercase alphabet and move up the last 4 bands to 4 threads below turquoise band. Center and stitch name on baseline, using DMC #334 and uppercase letters from *Elegant Victorians* Alphabet (p. 62) omitting backstitching from letters.

2. Trim design fabric ¼" beyond design at sides and 2¾" beyond at top and bottom. Zigzag-stitch edges.

3. Using design fabric as pattern, cut interfacing; fuse to back of design fabric, following manufacturer's instructions.

4. Cut green fabric (backing) 1" wider than and same length as design unit.

5. With right sides facing and matching edges, sew design unit to backing along sides, using ¼" seam allowance. Turn and press (seam lines roll toward design fabric and backing forms ¼" edging).

6. Zigzag-stitch top and bottom edges through all layers. For casings, turn zigzagged edges to back 1¾". Fold corners under approx. 1"; slip-stitch edges to backing.

7. Insert hardware.▲

HEART ORNAMENT OR WREATH HOLDER

MATERIALS

- 5"-sq. Natural linen (28-ct.)
- Floss for motif (see key)
- 4"-sq. **each** polyester fleece and medium-weight cardboard
- 12" of ⅛"-dia. premade dark red piping
- Tracing paper
- Tacky glue
- Hot glue gun
- Sandpaper (#400)
- **For ornament only**—4" of ⅛"-W dark red satin ribbon and tin heart with 3¼"-W design area
- **For wreath holder only**—tin wreath holder with 3¼"-W design area

INSTRUCTIONS

1. Holding tracing paper over tin heart, trace interior of scalloped edge with thumbnail. To make pattern, cut along impression.

2. Center and trace pattern lightly onto back of linen. Sew running stitches on traced line.

3. Using 3 strands of floss for cross-stitch, stitch ornament or wreath holder motif from cranberry variation of *Colonial Heritage Sampler* over 2 threads on linen, aligning blue dot on chart with center of linen; continue stitching 2 squares beyond running-stitch line. For ornament, omit saying and chain border at point of heart and move floral motif to within 2 threads of yellow band. For wreath holder, omit alphabet and motifs above upper border; center and stitch "welcome" on baseline, using lowercase alphabet and DMC #368 and #367.

4. Use pattern to cut fleece and cardboard; glue together.

5. Trace pattern onto back of design fabric (design centered). Trim fabric 1" beyond line.

6. Center design over fleece unit; pull edges to cardboard back and glue.

7. Glue flat edge of piping around back edge of design unit, overlapping ends at notch of heart.

8. For ornament, fold ribbon in half; glue ends to back of design unit at notch of heart.

9. Sand front of tin heart

or wreath holder. Hot-glue design unit into place.♠

LAMP TRIM

MATERIALS

- 13"x4" Natural linen (28-ct.)
- Floss for motif (see key)
- 13"x4" lightweight fusible interfacing
- ⅛ yd. dark red fabric
- Tin hurricane lamp base with 9⅝" circumference
- ¼"x¾" white Velcro®
- Sewing thread

INSTRUCTIONS

1. Beginning 1½" from left end of design fabric and centering top to bottom, stitch lamp motif from cranberry variation of *Colonial Heritage Sampler* over 2 threads on linen, using 3 strands of floss for cross-stitch. Repeat motif until design is approx. 9¾" wide.

2. Fuse interfacing to back of design fabric, following manufacturer's instructions.

3. Trim design unit ¾" beyond design at ends and ⅜" beyond design at top and bottom.

4. Cut red fabric (backing) 2⅜"W x length of design unit. With right sides facing and matching long edges, sew design unit and backing together,

using ¼" seam allowance. Turn and press (seam lines roll toward design and backing forms ¼" edging).

5. Turn ends of design unit into tube evenly so ends overlap ¼" when wrapped around lamp base; slip-stitch ends.

6. Slip-stitch half of Velcro to front of design unit at one end and remaining half to back of design unit at opposite end. Attach trim to lamp.♠

BASKET BAND

MATERIALS

- Natural linen (28-ct.), 4¼"-W x circumference of basket plus 4"
- Floss for motif (see key)
- Lightweight fusible interfacing, size of design fabric
- ¼ yd. dark red fabric
- Basket with at least 3"-H straight side
- 2" of ¾"-W white Velcro®
- Sewing thread

INSTRUCTIONS

1. Using 3 strands of floss for cross-stitch and substituting DMC #816 for top and bottom borders, stitch basket band motif from cranberry variation of *Colonial Heritage Sampler* over 2 threads on linen. Begin 2" from left end of fabric and center top to bottom; continue design to

within 2" of opposite end.

2. Fuse interfacing to back of design fabric, following manufacturer's instructions.

3. Trim 1" from all sides of design unit. Cut dark red fabric (backing) 3¾"W x length of design unit.

4. With right sides facing and using ⅜" seam allowance, sew long edges of design unit and backing; turn and press (seam lines roll toward design fabric and backing forms ⅜" edging).

5. Press remaining raw edges into tube ¼" and slip-stitch ends closed.

6. Slip-stitch half of Velcro to front of design unit at one end and remaining half to back of design unit at opposite end. Attach trim to basket.♠

SWEATER

MATERIALS

- Ecru cotton sweater
- Size 18 tapestry needle
- Floss for motif (see key)

INSTRUCTIONS

1. Using 6 strands of floss for duplicate stitch, stitch sweater motif from cranberry variation of *Colonial Heritage Sampler* across front of sweater from side seam to side seam, with top of design 2½" below center bottom edge of neckband.♠

HOLIDAY
SLEIGH RIDE

Designed by Jorja Hernandez

As Winter approaches, do your

thoughts drift to images of horse-drawn sleighs

journeying through landscapes of freshly fallen snow?

What better time to reflect on these images than Christmas?

This year you can capture all the beauty and excitement

of a sleigh ride by creating a picturesque

stocking and ornament.

This decorative wreath displays a memorable

image of wintertime and will surely become an

integral part of your Christmas decorating.

STOCKING

MATERIALS

- 18½"x7½" Forget-Me-Not Blue Aida 14
- Floss listed in chart key
- 16½"x5½" lightweight fusible interfacing
- ¼ yd. **each** red and white fabric
- ¾ yd. green print fabric
- ½ yd. green fabric
- 1½ yds. of ³⁄₁₆"-dia. cotton cord
- Sewing thread
- Graph paper

INSTRUCTIONS

USE ½" SEAM ALLOWANCE.

1. Referring to Fig. 1, stitch *Holiday Sleigh Ride* on Aida using 3 strands of floss for cross-stitch and centering name on baseline. Trim 1" from all sides

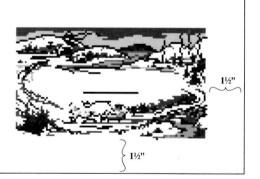

Figure 1

of design fabric. Using design fabric as pattern, cut white fabric (backing).

2. Fuse interfacing to back of design fabric, following manufacturer's instructions. With right sides facing, sew short

edges of design unit together; trim seam and turn.

3. With right sides facing, sew short edges of backing together; trim seams.

4. Cut and piece red fabric to make 2"x16½" bias strip. Cut 16½" length of cord. Using strip and cord, make piping; trim seam allowance to ½".

5. With raw edges even, baste piping to right side of design unit along bottom edge, overlapping ends at center back.

6. With right sides facing, sew design unit and backing together along bottom edge; trim seam and turn.

7. Using graph paper, enlarge Stocking Pattern A (p. 101); cut 2 each from green print and green fabric.

8. Cut and piece remaining green print fabric into 2"x36" and 1½"x5" bias strips. Using longer strip and remaining cotton cord, make piping. Trim piping seam allowance to ½".

9. With raw edges even and beginning 2" below top edge, baste piping to right side of one green print piece, along sides and foot, ending approx. 2" from top edge (Fig. 2).

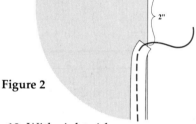

Figure 2

10. With right sides facing, sew green print (stocking) pieces together along sides and foot. Clip curves and turn.

11. Sew green fabric (lining) pieces together along sides and foot; leave 5" opening along one side. Trim seam allowance; clip curves.

12. For hanger, fold 5" bias strip in half lengthwise; sew long edge. Trim seam to ¼", turn, and press.

13. Fold hanger in half; sew to right side of lining back adjacent to back seam (with raw edges even).

14. With wrong side of cuff facing right side of green print and aligning seam of cuff with back seam of stocking unit, baste cuff to stocking unit around top edge.

15. Insert cuff unit into lining, right sides facing; sew together around top edge. Trim seam and turn. Slip-stitch opening in lining closed.▲

ORNAMENT

MATERIALS

- 5"-sq. Forget-Me-Not Blue Aida 14
- Floss for motif (see key)
- ¼ yd. red fabric
- 5"-sq. medium-weight cardboard
- ¼ yd. of ³⁄₁₆"-dia. cotton cord
- 2½"x1⅞" oval Stik'N Puff
- 10" of ⅛"-W red satin ribbon
- Tacky glue

INSTRUCTIONS

1. Lightly trace Stik'N Puff onto back of Aida. Aligning blue dot on chart with center of traced area, stitch sleigh motif from *Holiday Sleigh Ride*, using 3 strands of floss for cross-stitch. Continue stitching 2 squares beyond traced line.

2. Trace Stik'N Puff onto back of red fabric (backing) and cardboard. Trim design fabric and red fabric 1" beyond traced line. Cut cardboard along line.

3. Center foam side of Stik'N Puff over back of design; remove backing paper. Press Stik'N Puff firmly against fabric. Pull fabric edges onto adhesive backing. Glue where edges overlap.

Continued on page 51

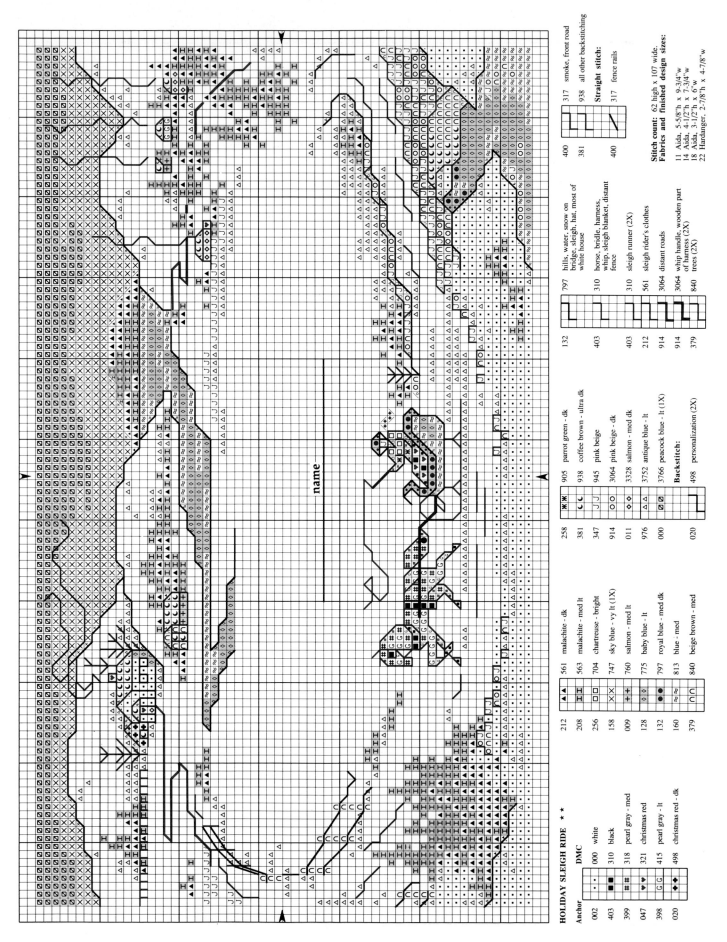

HOLIDAY SLEIGH RIDE ★ ★

Anchor	DMC	
002	000	white
403	310	black
399	318	pearl gray - med
047	321	christmas red
398	415	pearl gray - lt
020	498	christmas red - dk

212	561	malachite - dk
208	563	malachite - med lt
256	704	chartreuse - bright
158	747	sky blue - vy lt (1X)
009	760	salmon - med lt
128	775	baby blue - lt
132	797	royal blue - med dk
160	813	blue - med
379	840	beige brown - med

258	905	parrot green - dk
381	938	coffee brown - ultra dk
347	945	pink beige
914	3064	pink beige - dk
011	3328	salmon - med dk
976	3752	antique blue - lt
000	3766	peacock blue - lt (1X)

Backstitch:

020	498	personalization (2X)

132	797	hills, water, snow on bridge, sleigh, sleigh, hat, most of white house
403	310	horse, bridle, harness, whip, sleigh blanket, distant fence
403	310	sleigh runner (2X)
212	561	sleigh rider's clothes
914	3064	distant roads
914	3064	whip handle, wooden part of harness (2X)
379	840	trees (2X)

400	317	smoke, front road
381	938	all other backstitching

Straight stitch:

400	317	fence rails

Stitch count: 62 high x 107 wide.
Fabrics and finished design sizes:
11 Aida, 5-5/8"h x 9-3/4"w
14 Aida, 4-1/2"h x 7-3/4"w
18 Aida, 3-1/2"h x 6"w
22 Hardanger, 2-7/8"h x 4-7/8"w

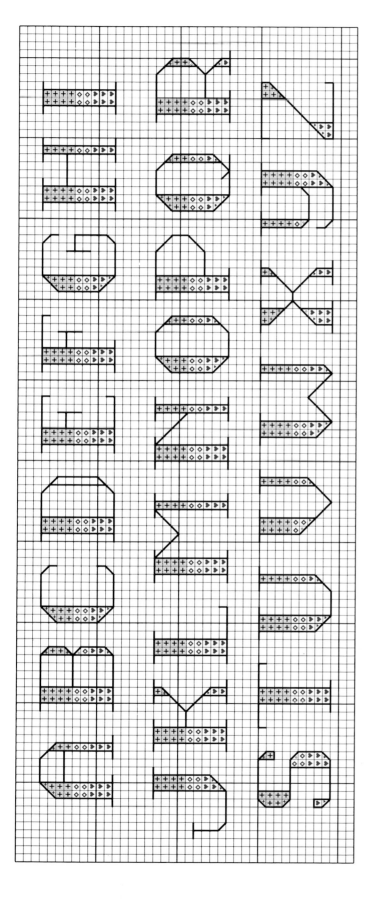

4. Center cardboard over backing fabric, pull edges to back, and glue.

5. Cut and piece remaining red fabric into 2"x9" bias strip. Using strip and cord, make piping; trim seam allowance to ½".

6. Glue piping around back of design unit; overlap ends at top.

7. Cut 3" of ribbon; fold in half. Glue raw ends to center top back of design unit.

8. Glue design and backing units together.

9. Tie remaining ribbon into 1"-W bow; trim ends diagonally. Glue bow to front of design unit at top edge (see photo).▲

WREATH ADORNMENT

MATERIALS

- 10⅝"x7½" Forget-Me-Not Blue Aida 14
- Floss listed in chart key
- ¼ yd. red fabric
- 25" of ³⁄₁₆"-dia. cotton cord
- 1 yd. of ¼"-W red satin ribbon
- Polyester fiberfill
- Evergreen wreath
- Sewing thread

INSTRUCTIONS

USE ½" SEAM ALLOWANCE.

1. Center and stitch *Holiday Sleigh Ride* on Aida using 3 strands of floss for cross-stitch. Center and stitch last name on baseline.

2. Trim design fabric ½" beyond design on all sides. Using design fabric as pattern, cut red fabric (backing).

3. Cut and piece remaining red fabric into 2"x25" bias strip. Using strip and cord make piping; trim seam allowance to ½".

4. With raw edges matching, baste piping around right side of design unit, overlapping ends at center bottom.

5. Cut ribbon in half; trim ends diagonally. Fold each ribbon length in half; baste folds of ribbons to one long edge of backing, 1¾" from short edges (Fig. 3).

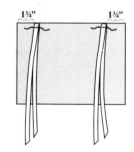

Figure 3

6. With right sides facing, sew design and backing units together, leaving 4" opening in bottom edge; do not catch ribbons in seams. Trim seams and turn.

7. Fill with fiberfill; slip-stitch opening closed.

8. Tie to wreath.▲

ELEGANT VICTORIANS

Designed by Barbara Baatz

Step back into historic England this

Christmas and enjoy the elaborate embellishments

of the Victorian era. The elegant floral motifs,

butterfly, cherub, and intricate patchwork

montages help produce a lavish stocking

and ornament that can turn any house

into a Christmas showplace.

These flatware holders, the candle trim,

and ornament will give your home a historic look

while turning your Christmas dinner

into an exquisite feast.

You've finished decorating your house.

Why stop there? This exquisite apron is the final

touch in creating the feeling of

an authentic Victorian Christmas.

"ELEGANT VICTORIANS" STOCKING

MATERIALS

- 15"x20" Black Aida 14
- Floss listed in chart key; additional floss skeins needed— white(3), 304(1), 894(1), 956(1), 3753(1)
- ½ yd. wine moiré faille
- ½ yd. wine cotton fabric
- 1⅛ yds. of ³⁄₁₆"-dia. cotton cord
- Sewing thread

INSTRUCTIONS

USE ½" SEAM ALLOWANCE.

1. Using 3 strands of floss for cross-stitch, center and stitch *Elegant Victorians* on Aida. Center and stitch name on baseline.

2. Sew running stitches around outer edge of design (see chart), allowing an extra ⅛" beyond design at top edge. Trim fabric ½" beyond running stitches.

3. Using design fabric as pattern, cut one stocking back from faille and 2 lining pieces from cotton fabric.

4. Cut and piece remaining faille into 2"x40" and 1½"x5" bias strips. Using longer strip and cord, make piping; trim seam to ½".

5. With raw edges even, baste piping to right side of design fabric along sides and foot.

6. With right sides together, sew stocking back to design unit; leave top open. Clip curves and turn right side out.

7. For hanger, fold shorter strip in half lengthwise; sew long edge. Trim seam to ¼", turn, and press.

8. Fold hanger in half; sew to right side of stocking back adjacent to piping (with raw edges even).

9. Sew lining pieces together along sides and foot; leave 5" opening in one side. Trim seam allowance to ¼"; clip curves.

10. Insert stocking unit into lining, right sides facing; sew together around top edge. Trim seam and turn. Slip-stitch opening in lining closed.▲

"VICTORIAN BOUQUET" STOCKING

MATERIALS

- 15"x20" Black Aida 14
- Floss for motif (see key); additional floss skeins needed— white(2), 894(1)
- ½ yd. wine moiré faille
- ½ yd. wine cotton fabric

- 1⅛ yds. of ³⁄₁₆"-dia. cotton cord
- Sewing thread

INSTRUCTIONS

USE ½" SEAM ALLOWANCE.

1. On Aida, center and outline stocking shape with running stitches (use chart as reference).

2. Using 3 strands of floss for cross-stitch, stitch Victorian bouquet motif as shown on *Elegant Victorians* (see photo). Center and stitch name on baseline.

3. Continue stripe pattern on stocking within running-stitch outline; continue stripes 2 squares beyond running stitches.

4. See Steps 2–10 of "Elegant Victorians" Stocking.▲

FLATWARE HOLDER

MATERIALS FOR ONE

- 9¼"x5" Black Aida 18
- Floss for motif (see key)
- ⅜ yd. moiré faille (pink for pansy, green for morning glory, wine for heart locket, or light blue for butterfly)
- ¼ yd. cotton fabric to match faille
- ⅛ yd. black cotton fabric

- ⅝ yd. of ⅛"-dia. cotton cord
- ¼ yd. of ½"-W flat, white lace
- Sewing thread
- Graph paper

INSTRUCTIONS

USE ½" SEAM ALLOWANCE, UNLESS OTHERWISE NOTED.

1. Referring to Fig. 1, sew running-stitch lines along vertical center of Aida and 1½" from right edge of fabric. Using 2 strands of floss for cross-stitch, center and stitch

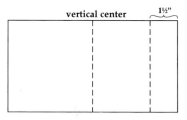

Figure 1

pansy, morning glory, heart locket, or butterfly motif from *Elegant Victorians* within running-stitch lines. Remove running stitches; trim 1" from all sides of design fabric. Using design fabric as pattern, cut black fabric (backing).

2. With right sides facing, sew short edges of design fabric together; trim

Continued on page 62

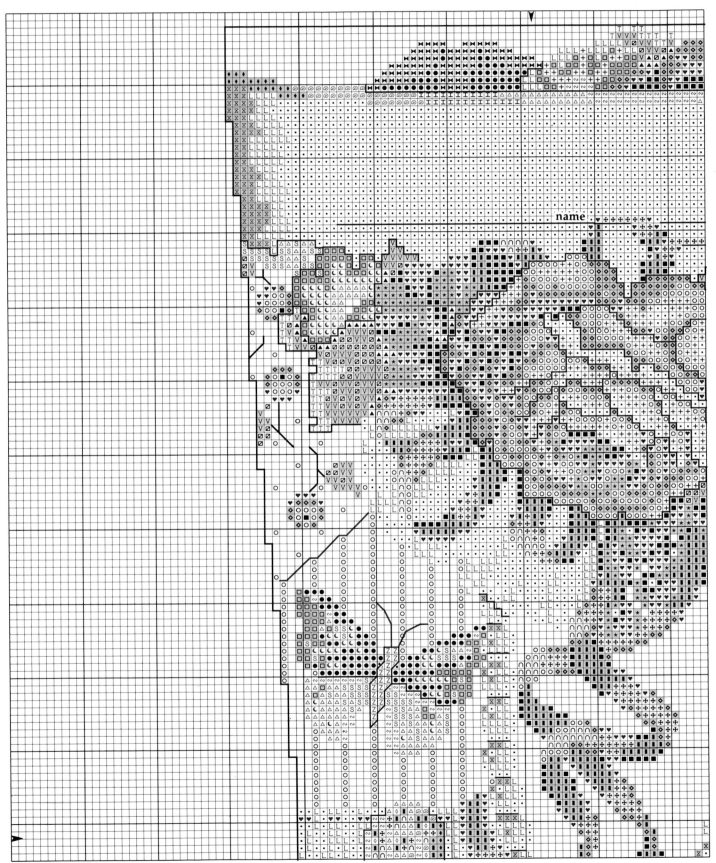

name

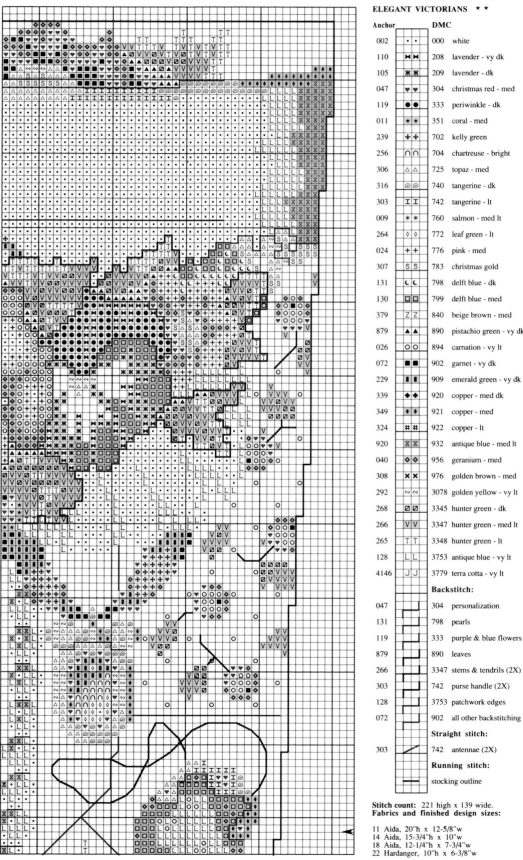

ELEGANT VICTORIANS ★ ★

Anchor		DMC	
002	· ·	000	white
110	Ӿ Ӿ	208	lavender - vy dk
105	Ӿ Ӿ	209	lavender - dk
047	♥ ♥	304	christmas red - med
119	● ●	333	periwinkle - dk
011	★ ★	351	coral - med
239	✚ ✚	702	kelly green
256	∩ ∩	704	chartreuse - bright
306	△ △	725	topaz - med
316	@ @	740	tangerine - dk
303	I I	742	tangerine - lt
009	* *	760	salmon - med lt
264	◇ ◇	772	leaf green - lt
024	+ +	776	pink - med
307	S S	783	christmas gold
131	C C	798	delft blue - dk
130	▢ ▢	799	delft blue - med
379	Z Z	840	beige brown - med
879	▲ ▲	890	pistachio green - vy dk
026	O O	894	carnation - vy lt
072	■ ■	902	garnet - vy dk
229	❚ ❚	909	emerald green - vy dk
339	✦ ✦	920	copper - med dk
349	◆ ◆	921	copper - med
324	# #	922	copper - lt
920	⊠ ⊠	932	antique blue - med lt
040	◇ ◇	956	geranium - med
308	✕ ✕	976	golden brown - med
292	∾ ∾	3078	golden yellow - vy lt
268	⊘ ⊘	3345	hunter green - dk
266	V V	3347	hunter green - med lt
265	T T	3348	hunter green - lt
128	L L	3753	antique blue - vy lt
4146	J J	3779	terra cotta - vy lt

Backstitch:

047		304	personalization
131		798	pearls
119		333	purple & blue flowers
879		890	leaves
266		3347	stems & tendrils (2X)
303		742	purse handle (2X)
128		3753	patchwork edges
072		902	all other backstitching

Straight stitch:

303		742	antennae (2X)

Running stitch:

		stocking outline

Stitch count: 221 high x 139 wide.
Fabrics and finished design sizes:

11 Aida, 20"h x 12-5/8"w
14 Aida, 15-3/4"h x 10"w
18 Aida, 12-1/4"h x 7-3/4"w
22 Hardanger, 10"h x 6-3/8"w

Shading at chart edge indicates chart area that overlaps.

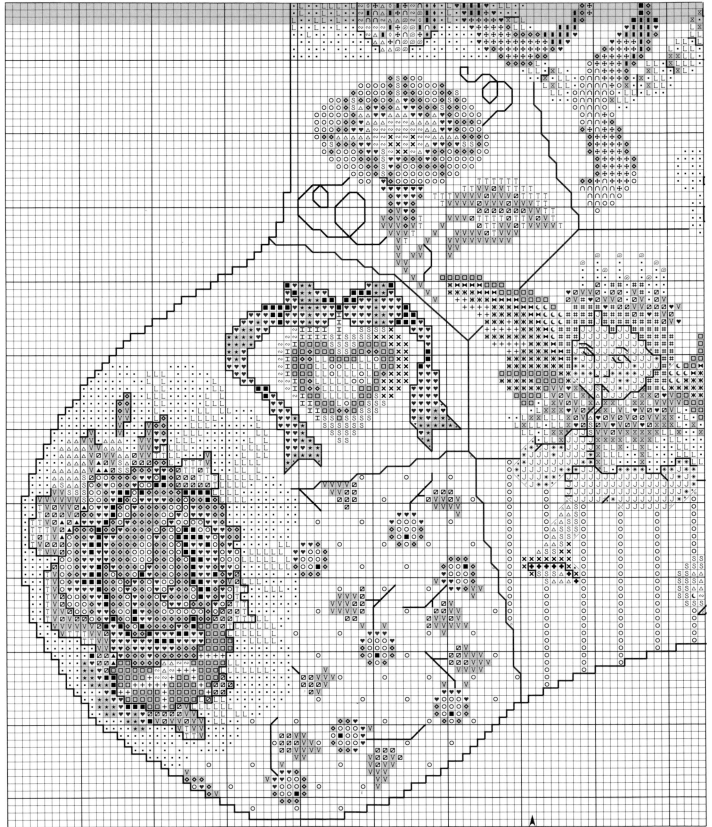

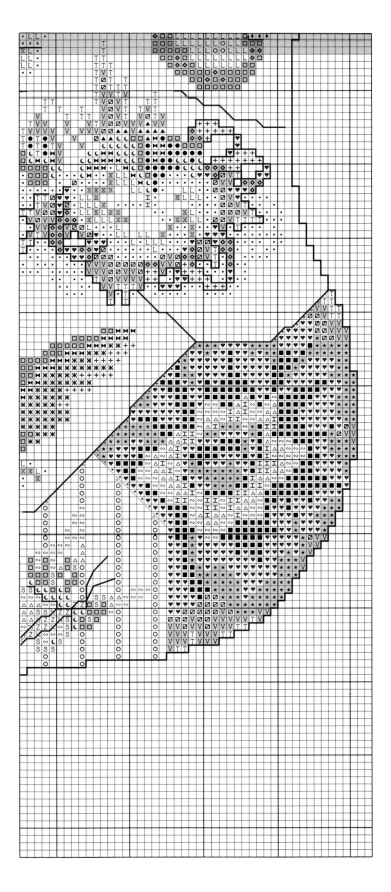

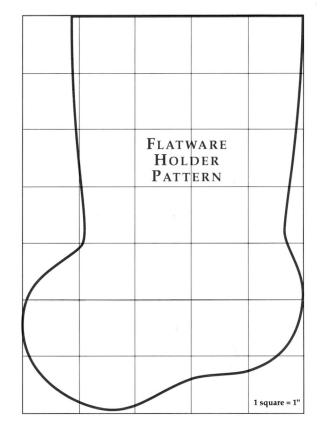

FLATWARE
HOLDER
PATTERN

1 square = 1"

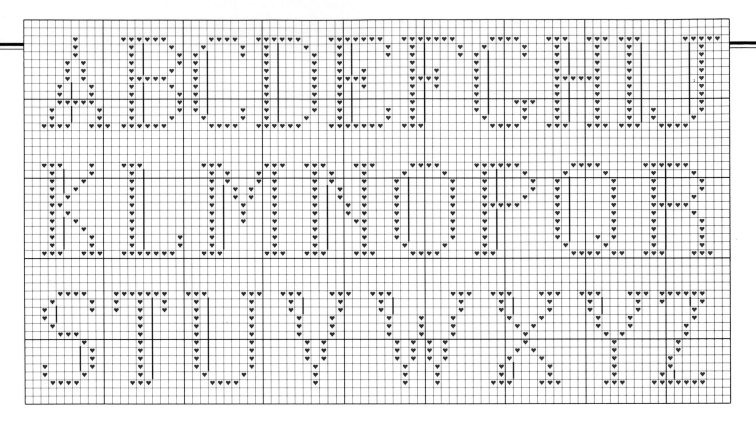

seam and turn. Repeat with backing fabric; do not turn.

3. Cut 2"x7⅜" bias strip from faille. Cut 7⅜" length of cord. Using strip and cord, make piping; trim seam allowance to ½".

4. With raw edges matching, baste piping to right side of design fabric along bottom edge, overlapping ends at center back.

5. With right sides facing, sew design unit and backing together along bottom edge; trim seam and turn.

6. Hand-sew flat edge of lace to back of cuff unit along bottom edge, overlapping ends at seam.

7. Using graph paper, enlarge Stocking Pattern C (p. 61); cut 2 each from faille and cotton fabric.

8. Cut and piece remain-

ing faille into 2"x13½" and ⅝"x4" bias strips. Using longer strip and remaining cord, make piping; trim seam allowance to ½".

9. With raw edges even and beginning 1" below top edge, baste piping to right side of one faille piece, along sides and foot, ending approx. 1" from top edge (Fig. 2).

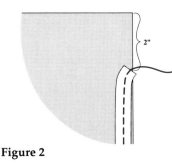

Figure 2

10. With right sides facing, sew faille pieces together along sides and foot. Clip curves and turn

right side out.

11. Sew cotton (lining) pieces together along sides and foot; leave 3" opening along one side. Trim seam allowance; clip curves.

12. For hanger, fold 4" bias strip in half lengthwise; sew long edge, using ⅛" seam allowance. Turn and press.

13. Fold hanger in half; sew to right side of lining back adjacent to back seam (with raw edges even).

14. With wrong side of cuff facing right side of faille and aligning seam of cuff with back seam of stocking unit, baste cuff to stocking unit around top edge.

15. Insert cuff unit into lining, right sides facing; sew together around top edge. Trim seam and turn. Slip-stitch opening in lining closed.♣

1⅝" below one short edge of fabric; center side to side.

Position Butterick pattern piece 1 atop design fabric with top edge of pattern ⅝" above top edge of design; center side to side. Cut design fabric along pattern at top and bottom and ⅜" beyond pattern at sides; zigzag-stitch edges.

2. Using Butterick pattern, cut white fabric and sew Apron A, substituting pattern piece 10 for piece 4 and using Apron C length; use design fabric as pattern to cut piece 1 from white fabric. Cut out pattern piece 9 from Apron B.

3. With right sides facing and using ⅝" seam allowance, sew design fabric and piece 1 together along top; trim seams and turn. Construct Apron, using design unit for piece 1 and substituting Battenburg lace for ¾"-W flat lace on ruffle. Use piece 9 to make ruffle, referring to Apron C instructions.▲

CANDLE ADORNMENT

MATERIALS

- •4"-sq. Black Aida 18
- •Floss for motif (see key)
- •4"-sq. burgundy fabric
- •5" of ³⁄₁₆"-W silver Bendable Ribbon™
- •Needlework Finisher
- •Small flat paint brush
- •Small, sharp scissors

INSTRUCTIONS

1. Using 2 strands of floss for cross-stitch, center and stitch small rose and leaves motif from *Elegant Victorians* on Aida.

2. Make two ³⁄₁₆"-W cuts ½" apart in center of burgundy fabric (Fig. 3).

Figure 3

Insert ribbon into one cut and bring it out at the other so that ½" protrudes.

3. Coat back of design with Needlework Finisher. Immediately position wrong side of backing fabric over still-wet back of design, with cuts centered over design; smooth out air bubbles. Apply Needlework Finisher to right side of backing; let dry.

4. Cut out design one square beyond stitching.

5. Bend ½" end of ribbon back toward opposite cut. Twist long end of ribbon into a loop to fit diameter of candle.▲

ORNAMENT

MATERIALS

- •6"x5" Black Aida 14
- •Floss for motif (see key)
- •6"x5" black fabric
- •5¼" of 2½"-W lavender moiré taffeta ribbon
- •6" of ¼"-W lavender satin ribbon
- •Small, sharp scissors
- •Sewing thread
- •Needlework Finisher
- •Tacky glue

INSTRUCTIONS

1. Using 3 strands of floss for cross-stitch, center and stitch angel motif from *Elegant Victorians* on Aida, omitting wings.

2. Coat back of design with Needlework Finisher. Immediately position wrong side of backing fabric over still-wet back of design; smooth out air bubbles. Apply coat of Needlework Finisher to right side of backing; let dry.

3. For "wings" trim and round-off ends of 2½"-W ribbon. Sew gathering stitches along vertical center of ribbon; gather ribbon to approx. ⅜" in center.

4. Cut 1" length of ¼"-W ribbon. Wrap length around center of 2½"-W ribbon, tacking ends at back. Fold remaining length of ¼"-W ribbon in half; tack ends to center back of 2½"-W ribbon.

5. Glue back of wing unit to center back of design unit.▲

CHRISTMAS KITTY

Designed by Jorja Hernandez

Here we have the mischievous family cat

"innocently" pulling the garland off your holiday tree.

Maybe it was an accident. Or maybe somebody wants a

little attention. This charming design makes an

engaging stocking or pair of ornaments that can be

enjoyed by the whole family. If you put a rubber

mouse in the stocking, your Christmas morning

might just go a little smoother.

What would Christmas be without

the family pet? Show your affection for your cat by

stitching this endearing design on a pillow and

displaying it proudly in your home.

STOCKING

MATERIALS

- 18¼"x7½" Light Oatmeal Fiddler's Lite 14
- Floss listed in chart key; additional floss skeins needed—white(2)
- ¼ yd. beige cotton fabric
- ½ yd. red and green plaid taffeta
- ½ yd. green cotton fabric
- ½ yd. green taffeta
- 2 yds. of ³⁄₁₆"-dia. cotton cord
- Sewing thread
- Graph paper

INSTRUCTIONS

USE ½" SEAM ALLOWANCE.

1. Referring to Fig. 1, stitch *Christmas Kitty* on Fiddler's Lite, using 3 strands of floss for cross-stitch and centering name on baseline. Trim 1" from all sides of design fabric. Using design fabric as

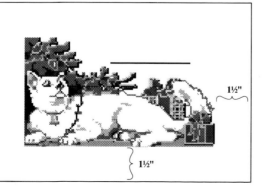

Figure 1

pattern, cut beige fabric (backing).

2. With right sides facing, sew short edges of design fabric together; trim seam and turn.

3. With right sides facing, sew short edges of backing together; trim seams.

4. Cut and piece two 2"x16¼" bias strips from green taffeta. Cut two 16¼" lengths cotton cord. Using strips and cord, make piping; trim seam allowance to ½". With raw edges matching, baste piping around right side of design unit along top and bottom edges, overlapping ends at seam.

5. With right sides facing, sew design unit and backing together along bottom edge; trim seam and turn.

6. Using graph paper, enlarge Stocking Pattern A (p. 101); cut 2 each from plaid taffeta and green cotton fabric.

7. Cut and piece remaining green taffeta into 2"x36"

and 1½"x5" bias strips. Using longer strip and cotton cord, make piping; trim seam allowance to ½".

8. With raw edges even and beginning 2" below top edge, baste piping to right side of one plaid taffeta piece, along sides and foot, ending approx. 2" from top edge (Fig. 2).

9. With right sides

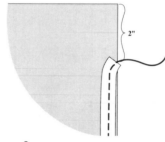

Figure 2

facing, sew plaid taffeta pieces together along sides and foot. Clip curves and turn right side out.

10. Sew green cotton (lining) pieces together along sides and foot; leave 5" opening along one side. Trim seam allowance; clip curves.

11. For hanger, fold 5" bias strip in half lengthwise; sew long edge. Trim seam to ¼", turn, and press.

12. Fold hanger in half; sew to right side of lining back adjacent to back seam (with raw edges even).

13. With wrong side of cuff facing right side of taffeta and aligning seam of cuff with back seam of stocking unit, baste cuff to stocking unit around top edge.

14. Insert cuff unit into lining, right sides facing; sew together around top edge. Trim seam and turn. Slip-stitch opening in lining closed.♠

PILLOW

MATERIALS

- 10⅝"x7½" Light Oatmeal Fiddler's Lite 14
- Floss listed in chart key; additional floss skeins needed—white(2)
- ½ yd. red and green plaid taffeta
- ¼ yd. green taffeta
- ¾ yd. of ³⁄₁₆"-dia. cotton cord
- Polyester fiberfill

INSTRUCTIONS

1. Using 3 strands of floss for cross-stitch, center and stitch *Christmas Kitty* on Fiddler's Lite. Center and stitch "Noel" on baseline, using *Elegant Victorians* Alphabet (p. 62).

2. Trim design fabric ½" beyond design on all sides. Cut plaid taffeta (backing) to match.

3. Cut and piece green taffeta to make 2"x24½" bias strip. Using strip and cord, make piping; trim seam allowance to ½".

4. With raw edges matching, baste piping

Continued on page 69

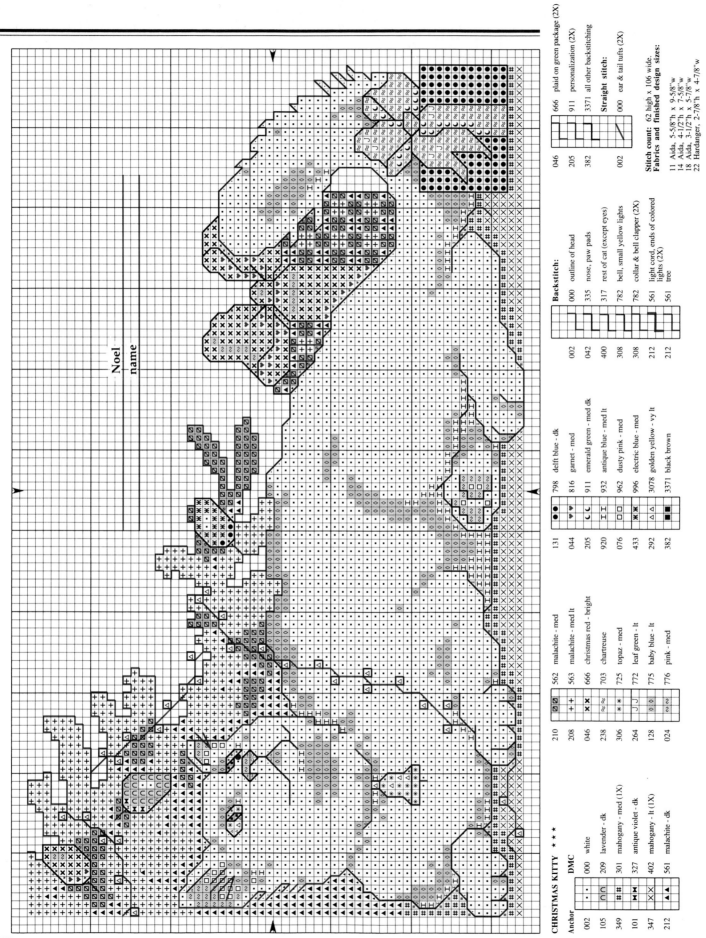

CHRISTMAS KITTY ★ ★ ★

Anchor	DMC					
002	·	000	white
105	∪	209	lavender - dk
349	#	301	mahogany - med (1X)
101	✕	327	antique violet - dk
347	✕	402	mahogany - lt (1X)
212	▲	561	malachite - dk

210	▨	562	malachite - med
208	+	563	malachite - med lt
046	✕	666	christmas red - bright
238	≈	703	chartreuse
306	✳	725	topaz - med
264	⌡⌡	772	leaf green - lt
128	◇	775	baby blue - lt
024	◇◇	776	pink - med

131	●	798	delft blue - dk
044	▶	816	garnet - med
205	⌣	911	emerald green - med dk
920	H	932	antique blue - med lt
076	▢	962	dusty pink - med
433	✳✳	996	electric blue - med
292	◁	3078	golden yellow - vy lt
382	■	3371	black brown

Backstitch:

000	outline of head
002	nose, paw pads
042	rest of cat (except eyes)
400	bell, small yellow lights
308	bell & bell clapper (2X)
308	light cord, ends of colored
212	lights (2X)
212	tree

046	plaid on green package (2X)
205	personalization (2X)
382	all other backstitching

Straight stitch:

| 000 | ear & tail tufts (2X) |

Stitch count: 62 high x 106 wide.
Fabrics and finished design sizes:
11 Aida, 5-5/8"h x 9-5/8"w
14 Aida, 4-1/2"h x 7-5/8"w
18 Aida, 3-1/2"h x 5-7/8"w
22 Hardanger, 2-7/8"h x 4-7/8"w

Noel
name

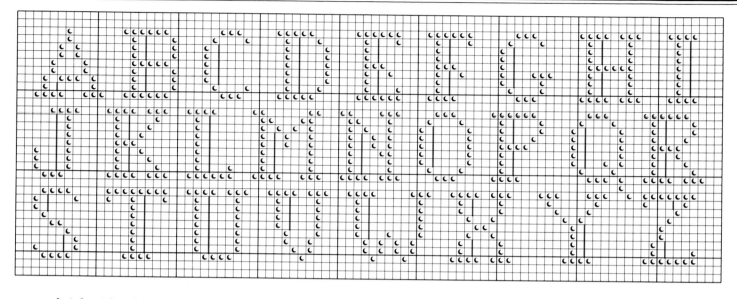

around right side of design fabric, overlapping ends at center bottom.

5. Cut and piece remaining plaid taffeta to make 6"x79" bias strip (ruffle). With right sides facing, sew short sides of strip together, making a loop; press seam open.

6. Fold ruffle in half lengthwise, wrong sides facing; press. Sew two rows of gathering stitches, ¼" and ⅜" from raw edge. Gather ruffle to pillow circumference.

7. With right sides facing and matching raw edges, baste ruffle around design unit, spreading gathers evenly.

8. With right sides facing, sew backing to design unit, leaving 5" opening at bottom; trim seams slightly at corners and turn.

9. Fill design unit firmly with fiberfill. Slip-stitch opening closed.▲

ORNAMENT

MATERIALS

- Light Oatmeal Fiddler's Lite 14 (5"-sq. for package **or** 6"x7" for kitty)
- Floss for motif (see key)
- ¼ yd. **each** red and green plaid taffeta and green taffeta fabric
- 4"-sq. medium-weight cardboard
- ⅜ yd. of ³⁄₁₆"-dia. cotton cord
- Stik'N Puff (2¼"-dia. round for package **or** 2⅝"x3⅝" oval for kitty)
- 4" of ¼"-W green satin ribbon
- Tacky glue
- Sewing thread

INSTRUCTIONS

1. Use 3 strands of floss for cross-stitch. For package motif, center and stitch package motif from

Christmas Kitty on Fiddler's Lite. For kitty motif, lightly trace Stik'N Puff onto back of Fiddler's Lite. Stitch kitty motif from *Christmas Kitty*, aligning blue dot on chart with center of traced area. Continue stitching 2 squares beyond traced line.

2. Trace Stik'N Puff onto back of design fabric (design centered), green taffeta (backing), and cardboard. Trim fabrics 1" beyond traced line. Cut cardboard along line.

3. Center foam side of Stik'N Puff over back of design; remove backing paper. Press Stik'N Puff firmly against fabric. Pull fabric edges onto adhesive backing. Glue where edges overlap.

4. Center cardboard over backing fabric, pull edges to back, and glue.

5. Cut and piece remaining green taffeta to make bias strip (2"x9½" for package **or** 2"x12½" for

kitty). Cut cord to match length of bias strip. Using strip and cord, make piping; trim piping seam allowance to ½".

6. Glue flat edge of piping around back edge of design unit, overlapping ends at top.

7. Cut and piece plaid taffeta to make bias strip (2"x20" for package **or** 2"x24" for kitty). With right sides facing, sew short sides of strip together, making a loop; press seam open.

8. Fold strip in half lengthwise, wrong sides facing; press. Sew two rows of gathering stitches, beginning ⅛" from raw edge. Gather to Stik'N Puff circumference. Glue gathered edge of ruffle to back edge of design unit.

9. Fold ribbon in half; glue raw ends to center top back of design unit.

10. Glue design and backing units together.▲

BABY'S FIRST CHRISTMAS

Designed by Linda Gillum

O ne of life's most precious gifts is

a newborn child. And baby's first Christmas

is one of the most memorable times of a parent's life.

These adorable designs can help you create mementos

to celebrate this joyful occasion.

A teddy bear tucked up amid

its favorite toys—who can resist the sight? Stitch it for

a girl or boy on a stocking, bib, and ornament. Then repeat

the theme on a bonnet, T-shirt, and gown. One day your

child might even experience the same enjoyment by

passing them on to his or her child.

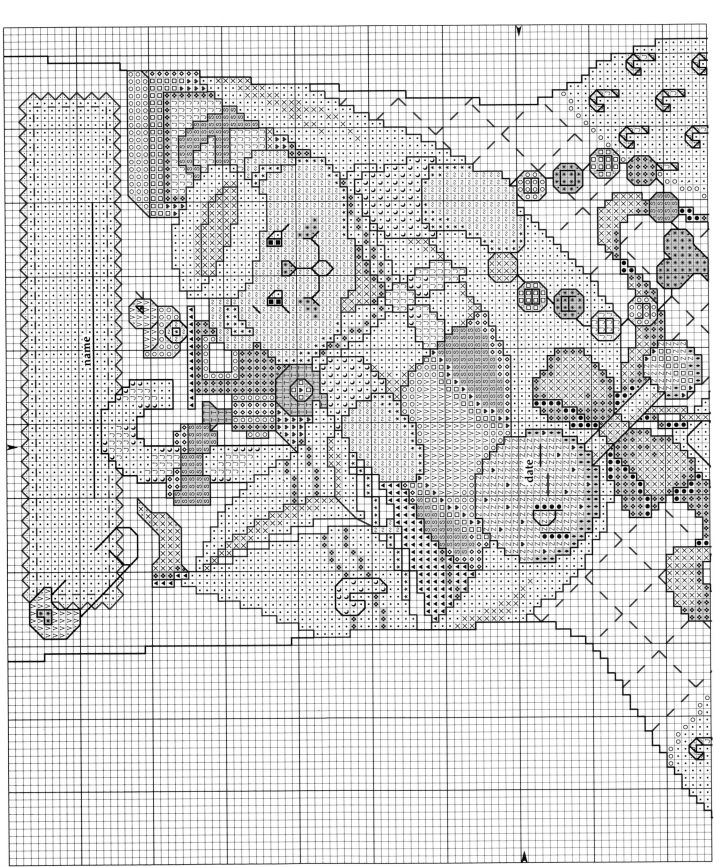

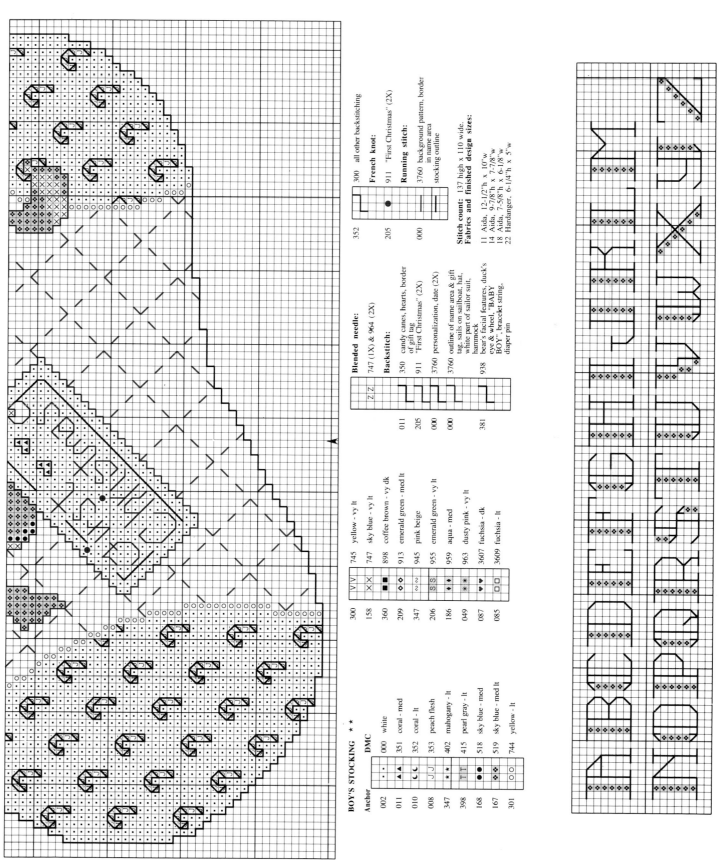

French knot:

| 352 | 300 | all other backstitching |
| 205 | 911 | "First Christmas" (2X) |

Running stitch:

| 000 | 3760 | background pattern, border in name area stocking outline |

Blended needle:

| | 747 (1X) & 964 (2X) |

Backstitch:

350		candy canes, hearts, border of gift tag
011		
205	911	"First Christmas" (2X)
000	3760	personalization, date (2X)
000	3760	outline of name area & gift tag, sails on sailboat, hat, white part of sailor suit, hammock
381	938	bear's facial features, duck's eye & wheel, "BABY BOY", bracelet string, diaper pin

Stitch count: 137 high x 110 wide.
Fabrics and finished design sizes:
11 Aida, 12-1/2"h x 10"w
14 Aida, 9-7/8"h x 7-7/8"w
18 Aida, 7-5/8"h x 6-1/8"w
22 Hardanger, 6-1/4"h x 5"w

BOY'S STOCKING ★★

Anchor	DMC	
002	000	white
011	351	coral - med
010	352	coral - lt
008	353	peach flesh
347	402	mahogany - lt
398	415	pearl gray - lt
168	518	sky blue - med
167	519	sky blue - med lt
301	744	yellow - lt
300	745	yellow - vy lt
158	747	sky blue - vy lt
360	898	coffee brown - vy dk
209	913	emerald green - med lt
347	945	pink beige
206	955	emerald green - vy lt
186	959	aqua - med
049	963	dusty pink - vy lt
087	3607	fuchsia - dk
085	3609	fuchsia - lt

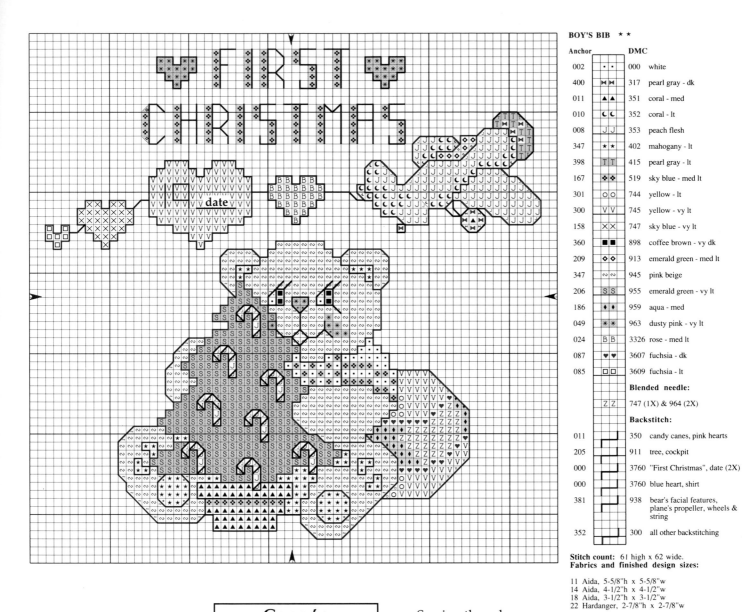

BOY'S BIB ★ ★

Anchor		DMC	
002	· ·	000	white
400	⋈ ⋈	317	pearl gray - dk
011	▲ ▲	351	coral - med
010	C C	352	coral - lt
008	J J	353	peach flesh
347	★ ★	402	mahogany - lt
398	T T	415	pearl gray - lt
167	❖ ❖	519	sky blue - med lt
301	o o	744	yellow - lt
300	V V	745	yellow - vy lt
158	X X	747	sky blue - vy lt
360	■ ■	898	coffee brown - vy dk
209	◇ ◇	913	emerald green - med lt
347	∾ ∾	945	pink beige
206	S S	955	emerald green - vy lt
186	◆ ◆	959	aqua - med
049	✳ ✳	963	dusty pink - vy lt
024	B B	3326	rose - med lt
087	♥ ♥	3607	fuchsia - dk
085	□ □	3609	fuchsia - lt

Blended needle:

	Z Z		747 (1X) & 964 (2X)

Backstitch:

011		350	candy canes, pink hearts
205		911	tree, cockpit
000		3760	"First Christmas", date (2X)
000		3760	blue heart, shirt
381		938	bear's facial features, plane's propeller, wheels & string
352		300	all other backstitching

Stitch count: 61 high x 62 wide.
Fabrics and finished design sizes:

11 Aida, 5-5/8"h x 5-5/8"w
14 Aida, 4-1/2"h x 4-1/2"w
18 Aida, 3-1/2"h x 3-1/2"w
22 Hardanger, 2-7/8"h x 2-7/8"w

GIRL'S STOCKING

- Sewing thread
- Tracing paper

MATERIALS

- 12"x14" Pink Aida 14
- Floss listed in chart key; additional floss skeins needed— white(4)
- ¾ yd. pink fabric
- 28" of ³⁄₁₆"-dia. cotton cord

INSTRUCTIONS

USE ½" SEAM ALLOWANCE.

1. Using 3 strands of floss for cross-stitch, center and stitch *Girl's Stocking* on Aida. Center and stitch child's name on baseline.

2. Sew running stitches around outer edge of design (see chart). Trim fabric ½" beyond running stitches.

3. Using design fabric as pattern, cut one stocking back and 2 lining pieces from pink fabric.

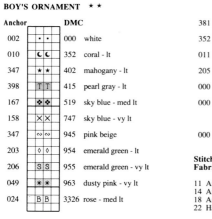

BOY'S ORNAMENT ★ ★

Anchor			DMC	
002	•	•	000	white
010	C	C	352	coral - lt
347	★	★	402	mahogany - lt
398	T	T	415	pearl gray - lt
167	❖	❖	519	sky blue - med lt
158	X	X	747	sky blue - vy lt
347	∾	∾	945	pink beige
203	◊	◊	954	emerald green - lt
206	S	S	955	emerald green - vy lt
049	✳	✳	963	dusty pink - vy lt
024	B	B	3326	rose - med lt

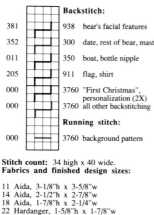

Backstitch:

381		938	bear's facial features
352		300	date, rest of bear, mast
011		350	boat, bottle nipple
205		911	flag, shirt
000		3760	"First Christmas", personalization (2X)
000		3760	all other backstitching

Running stitch:

000		3760	background pattern

Stitch count: 34 high x 40 wide.
Fabrics and finished design sizes:

11 Aida, 3-1/8"h x 3-5/8"w
14 Aida, 2-1/2"h x 2-7/8"w
18 Aida, 1-7/8"h x 2-1/4"w
22 Hardanger, 1-5/8"h x 1-7/8"w

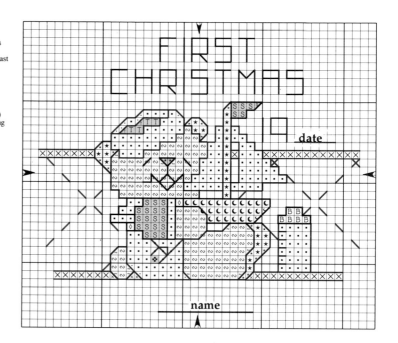

4. Cut and piece remaining pink fabric into 2"x28" and 1½"x5" bias strips. Using longer strip and cord, make piping; trim seam allowance to ½".

5. With raw edges even, baste piping to right side of design fabric along sides and foot.

6. With right sides together, sew stocking back to design unit; leave top open. Clip curves and turn right side out.

7. For hanger, fold shorter strip in half lengthwise; sew long edge. Trim seam to ¼", turn, and press.

8. Fold hanger in half; sew to right side of stocking back adjacent to piping (with raw edges even).

9. Sew lining pieces together along sides and foot; leave 5" opening in one side. Trim seam allowance to ¼"; clip curves.

10. Insert stocking unit into lining, right sides facing; sew together around top edge. Trim seam and turn. Slip-stitch opening in lining closed.▲

GIRL'S BIB

MATERIALS

•Premade bib with pink binding and White Aida-14 inset
•Floss listed in chart key

INSTRUCTIONS

1. Using 3 strands of floss for cross-stitch, center and stitch *Girl's Bib* on bib.▲

GIRL'S LARGE ORNAMENT

MATERIALS

•7"-sq. Pink Aida 14
•Floss for motif (see key)
•5"-sq. lightweight cardboard
•¼ yd. pink fabric
•15" of 1"-W gathered white eyelet
•15" of ³⁄₁₆"-dia. cotton cord
•4"-dia. round Stik'N Puff
•4" of ⅛"-W white grosgrain ribbon
•Tacky glue
•Sewing thread

INSTRUCTIONS

1. Using 3 strands of floss for cross-stitch, center and stitch bear with tree motif from *Girl's Bib* on Aida.

2. Trace Stik'N Puff shape onto back of design fabric (design centered), pink fabric (backing), and cardboard. Trim fabrics 1" beyond traced line. Cut cardboard along line.

3. Center foam side of Stik'N Puff over back of design fabric; remove backing paper. Press Stik'N Puff firmly against fabric. Pull fabric edges onto adhesive backing. Use glue where edges overlap.

Continued on next page

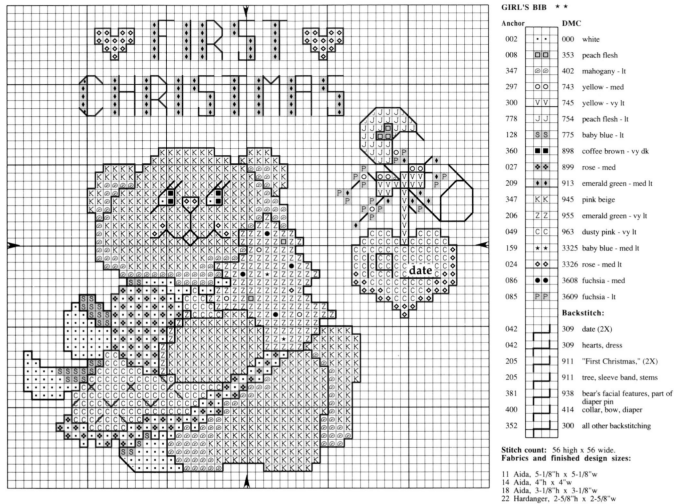

GIRL'S BIB ★ ★

Anchor		DMC	
002	· ·	000	white
008	⊡ ⊡	353	peach flesh
347	⊚ ⊚	402	mahogany - lt
297	○ ○	743	yellow - med
300	V V	745	yellow - vy lt
778	J J	754	peach flesh - lt
128	S S	775	baby blue - lt
360	■ ■	898	coffee brown - vy dk
027	❖ ❖	899	rose - med
209	♦ ♦	913	emerald green - med lt
347	K K	945	pink beige
206	Z Z	955	emerald green - vy lt
049	C C	963	dusty pink - vy lt
159	★ ★	3325	baby blue - med lt
024	◇ ◇	3326	rose - med lt
086	● ●	3608	fuchsia - med
085	P P	3609	fuchsia - lt

Backstitch:

042		309	date (2X)
042		309	hearts, dress
205		911	"First Christmas," (2X)
205		911	tree, sleeve band, stems
381		938	bear's facial features, part of diaper pin
400		414	collar, bow, diaper
352		300	all other backstitching

Stitch count: 56 high x 56 wide.
Fabrics and finished design sizes:

11 Aida, 5-1/8"h x 5-1/8"w
14 Aida, 4"h x 4"w
18 Aida, 3-1/8"h x 3-1/8"w
22 Hardanger, 2-5/8"h x 2-5/8"w

4. Cut and piece remaining pink fabric into 2"x15" bias strip. Using strip and cord, make piping; trim seam allowance to ½".

5. Glue flat edge of piping around back edge of design fabric, overlapping at top. Repeat with eyelet.

6. Fold ribbon in half. Glue raw ends to center top back of design unit.

7. Center cardboard over backing fabric; pull edges to back and glue. Glue design and backing units together.▲

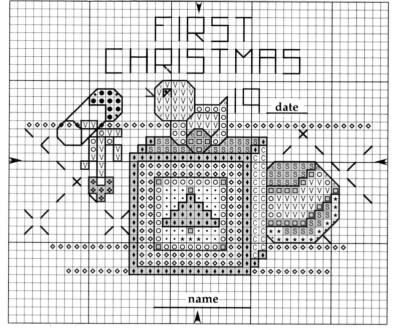

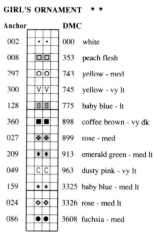

GIRL'S ORNAMENT ★ ★

Anchor		DMC	
002	· ·	000	white
008	□ □	353	peach flesh
297	○ ○	743	yellow - med
300	V V	745	yellow - vy lt
128	S S	775	baby blue - lt
360	■ ■	898	coffee brown - vy dk
027	✦ ✦	899	rose - med
209	♦ ♦	913	emerald green - med lt
049	C C	963	dusty pink - vy lt
159	★ ★	3325	baby blue - med lt
024	◇ ◇	3326	rose - med lt
086	● ●	3608	fuchsia - med

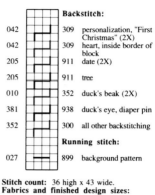

Backstitch:

042		309	personalization, "First Christmas" (2X)
042		309	heart, inside border of block
205		911	date (2X)
205		911	tree
010		352	duck's beak (2X)
381		938	duck's eye, diaper pin
352		300	all other backstitching

Running stitch:

027		899	background pattern

Stitch count: 36 high x 43 wide.
Fabrics and finished design sizes:

11 Aida, 3-3/8"h x 4"w
14 Aida, 2-5/8"h x 3-1/8"w
18 Aida, 2"h x 2-3/8"w
22 Hardanger, 1-5/8"h x 2"w

GIRL'S SMALL ORNAMENT

MATERIALS

- 6"-sq. Pink Aida 14
- Floss listed in chart key
- 2¾"-dia. **each** heavy and lightweight cardboard
- 4"-sq. polyester fleece
- ¼ yd. pink fabric
- 12" of 1"-W gathered white eyelet
- 12" of ³⁄₁₆"-dia. cotton cord

- 4" of ⅛"-W white grosgrain ribbon
- Tacky glue
- Sewing thread

INSTRUCTIONS

1. Using 3 strands of floss for cross-stitch, center and stitch *Girl's Ornament* on Aida.

2. Trace cardboard onto back of design fabric (design centered), pink fabric (backing), and fleece.

Trim fabrics 1" beyond traced line. Cut fleece along line. Glue fleece to heavy cardboard.

3. Center design fabric over fleece unit; pull edges to cardboard back and glue.

4. See Steps 3–6 for Girl's Large Ornament, making 2"x12" bias strip and using lightweight cardboard for backing.▲

Continued on page 82

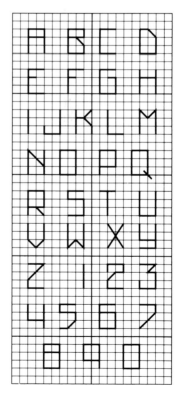

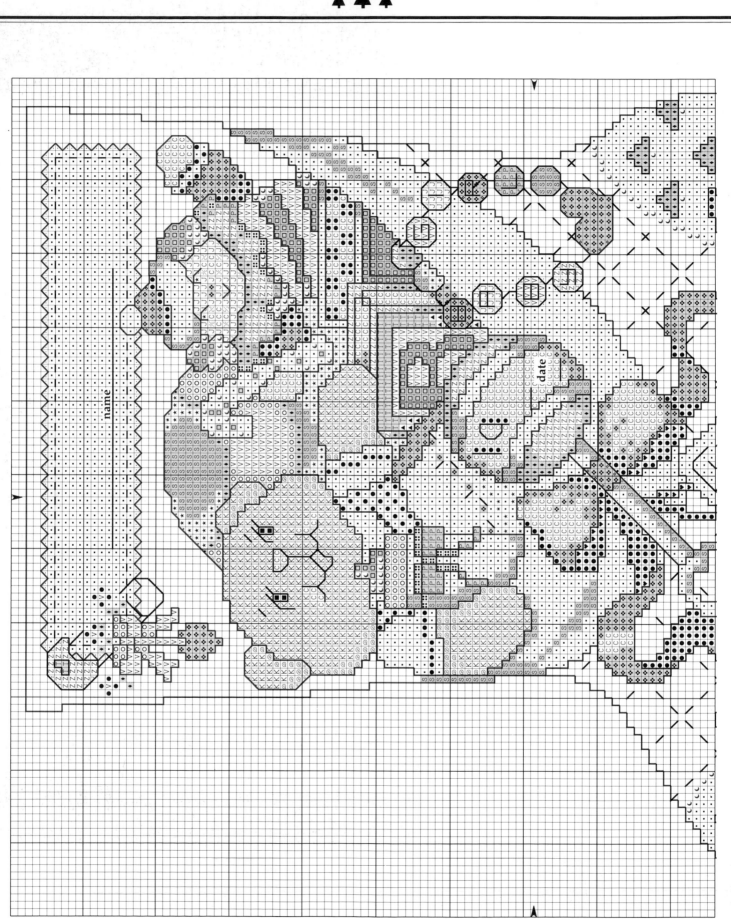

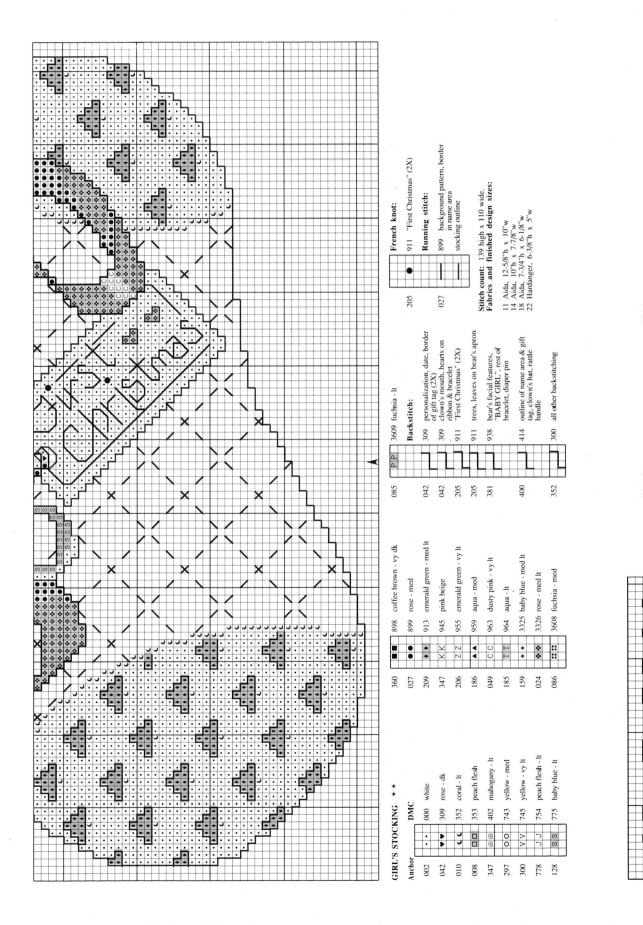

French knot:		
205	911	"First Christmas" (2X)

Running stitch:

027	899	background pattern, border in name area
		stocking outline

Stitch count: 139 high x 110 wide.
Fabrics and finished design sizes:
11 Aida, 12-5/8"h x 10"w
14 Aida, 10"h x 7-7/8"w
18 Aida, 7-3/4"h x 6-1/8"w
22 Hardanger, 6-3/8"h x 5"w

P.P.	3609	fuchsia - lt				
	Backstitch:					
085	309	personalization, date, border of gift tag (2X)				
042	309	clown's mouth, hearts on ribbon & bracelet				
042	911	"First Christmas" (2X)				
205	911	trees, leaves on bear's apron				
205	938	bear's facial features, "BABY GIRL", rest of bracelet, diaper pin				
381	414	outline of name area & gift tag, clown's hat, rattle handle				
400	300	all other backstitching				
352						

GIRL'S STOCKING ★ ★

Anchor			DMC		
360	■ ■	898	coffee brown - vy dk		
027	● ●	899	rose - med		
209	◆ ◆	913	emerald green - med lt		
347	K K	945	pink beige		
206	Z Z	955	emerald green - vy lt		
186	▲ ▲	959	aqua - med		
049	C C	963	dusty pink - vy lt		
185	T T	964	aqua - lt		
159	★ ★	3325	baby blue - med lt		
024	✣ ✣	3326	rose - med lt		
086	▦ ▦	3608	fuchsia - med		

Anchor			DMC		
002	· ·	000	white		
042	▶ ▼	309	rose - dk		
010	◖ ◖	352	coral - lt		
008	□ □	353	peach flesh		
347	@ @	402	mahogany - lt		
297	O O	743	yellow - med		
300	V V	745	yellow - vy lt		
778	J J	754	peach flesh - lt		
128	S S	775	baby blue - lt		

GOWN

MATERIALS

- White newborn gown
- 3"x4" of 14-ct. waste canvas
- Floss for motif (see key)
- Masking tape
- Sewing thread
- Tweezers

INSTRUCTIONS

1. Tape edges of waste canvas to prevent fraying. Position canvas on right front of gown with one edge even with lower edge of neckline; center side to side between armhole and center front of gown (Fig. 1). Baste canvas to gown front.

2. Using 3 strands of floss for cross-stitch, center and stitch diaper pin with bow from *Girl's Bib* on waste canvas; omit date.

3. When stitching is complete, remove basting threads and trim away tape. Wet the canvas. Using tweezers, pull individual canvas threads from under cross-stitches.▲

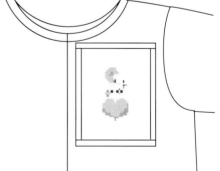

Figure 1

BONNET

MATERIALS

- White newborn bonnet
- 3" square of 14-ct. waste canvas
- Floss for motif (see key)
- Masking tape
- White sewing thread
- Tweezers

INSTRUCTIONS

1. See Steps 1 and 3 for Gown, centering canvas on one side of bonnet. Using 3 strands of floss for cross-stitch, center and stitch diaper pin with bow from *Girl's Stocking*.▲

BOY'S STOCKING

MATERIALS

- 12"x14" Light Blue Aida 14
- Floss listed in chart key; additional floss skeins needed—white(4)
- ¾ yd. light blue fabric
- 28" of ³⁄₁₆"-dia. cotton cord
- Sewing thread
- Tracing paper

INSTRUCTIONS

USE ½" SEAM ALLOWANCE.

1. Using 3 strands of floss for cross-stitch, center and stitch *Boy's Stocking* on Aida. Center and stitch child's name on baseline.

2. See Steps 2–10 for Girl's Stocking.▲

BOY'S BIB

MATERIALS

- Premade bib with light blue binding and White Aida-14 inset
- Floss listed in chart key

INSTRUCTIONS

1. Using 3 strands of floss for cross-stitch, center and stitch *Boy's Bib* on bib.▲

BOY'S LARGE ORNAMENT

MATERIALS

- 7"-sq. Light Blue Aida 14
- Floss for motif (see key)
- 5"-sq. lightweight cardboard
- ¼ yd. light blue fabric
- 15" of 1"-W gathered white eyelet
- 15" of ³⁄₁₆"-dia. cotton cord
- 4"-dia. round Stik'N Puff
- 4" of ⅛"-W white grosgrain ribbon
- Tacky glue
- Sewing thread

INSTRUCTIONS

1. Using 3 strands of floss for cross-stitch, center and stitch bear with tree motif from *Boy's Bib* on Aida.

2. See Steps 2–7 for Girl's Large Ornament, using

light blue fabric for backing.♣

BOY'S SMALL ORNAMENT

MATERIALS

- 6"-sq. Light Blue Aida 14
- Floss listed in chart key
- 2¾"-dia. **each** heavy and lightweight cardboard
- 4"-sq. polyester fleece
- ¼ yd. light blue fabric
- 12" of 1"-W gathered white eyelet
- 12" of ³⁄₁₆"-dia. cotton cord

- 4" of ⅛"-W white grosgrain ribbon
- Tacky glue
- Sewing thread

INSTRUCTIONS

1. Using 3 strands of floss for cross-stitch, center and stitch *Boy's Ornament* on Aida.

2. See Steps 2–4 for Girl's Small Ornament; use light blue fabric for backing.♣

T-SHIRT

MATERIALS

- White infant/toddler T-shirt

- 3" square of 14-ct. waste canvas
- Floss for motif (see key)
- Masking tape
- White sewing thread
- Tweezers

INSTRUCTIONS

1. Tape edges of waste canvas to prevent fraying. Position canvas on front of T-shirt with one edge even with lower edge of neckline; center side to side (Fig. 2). Baste canvas to T-shirt front.

2. Using 3 strands of floss for cross-stitch, center and stitch airplane motif

Figure 2

from *Boy's Bib* on waste canvas.

3. When stitching is complete, remove basting threads and trim away tape. Wet the canvas. Using tweezers, pull individual canvas threads from under cross-stitches.♣

CROSS-STITCH BASICS

PEACE HEART ★ ★			
Anchor		DMC	
387	♥♥	001 ecru	
890	▲▲	436 tan	
188	■■	943 teal	
Backstitch:			
403		310 bell (2X)	
20		498 outline	

CHART RATINGS	
EASY	★
EXPERIENCED	★★
SKILLED	★★★
EXPERT	★★★★

FLOSS/NEEDLES		
Fabric Count	Tapestry Needle Size	No. of Strands
11	24	3
14	24–26	2
18	26	2
22	26	1

Choose your chart
- Our keys show the skill level by the number of stars next to the title.

Use your key
- Cross-stitch colors, excluding specialty stitches, are listed in DMC numerical order. Project instructions specify if more than one skein of a color is needed and will note additional amounts.
- Specialty stitches are listed in the order worked; check for colors not listed above.
- Backstitches normally require one strand of floss; (2X) designates two strands, (3X) three, etc.
- Our keys designate white as 000 and ecru by 001.
- For linen-weave fabrics, the project instructions indicate whether to stitch over *one* or *two* threads.

1. Fold fabric to find center, and baste along fold lines. Zig-zag edges.

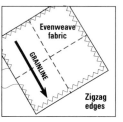

2. Cut floss into 15"–18" lengths and separate the strands. Recombine strands as needed.

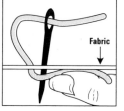

3. Push needle up through fabric. Hold loose end and pull thread through. Secure end with the first few stitches.

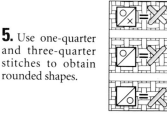

4. Make one cross-stitch for each symbol on chart (A). For horizontal rows, stitch across, then work back (B).

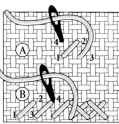

5. Use one-quarter and three-quarter stitches to obtain rounded shapes.

6. Add backstitches to outline and define.

Note: to end each color, weave floss through back of stitches.

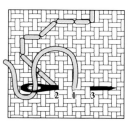

TEDDY BEAR SANTAS

Designed by Linda Gillum

What a delightful addition to Christmas morning!

Four teddy bears masquerade as Santa Claus,

bearing toys and Christmas trees. Each one embodies

the child-like whimsy and frolic that

everyone feels when they first wake up on

Christmas Day. Why not share the merriment

with someone else? The stocking and ornaments make

great gifts for family or friends.

I t's time for Christmas dinner.

This charming table runner, place mat, napkin,

and place card will help spread the fun

throughout your dining room.

What do you do with all the knick-knacks

that you accumulate every Christmas?

This collector's cabinet with a stitched inset

is an excellent way to display your

collectibles during the holiday season.

STOCKING

MATERIALS

- 20"x7¾" White Jobelan (28-ct.)
- Floss listed in chart key; additional floss skein needed—321(1)
- 18"x5¾" lightweight fusible interfacing
- ¼ yd. white fabric
- ½ yd. green print fabric
- ½ yd. green fabric
- ¼ yd. red pindot fabric
- ⅝ yd. of ³⁄₁₆"-dia. cotton cord
- Sewing thread
- Graph paper

INSTRUCTIONS

USE ½" SEAM ALLOWANCE, UNLESS OTHERWISE NOTED.

1. Using 3 strands of floss for cross-stitch and referring to Fig. 1, stitch *Teddy Bear Santas* over 2 threads on Jobelan, centering name on baseline and omitting hearts as necessary. Trim 1" from all sides

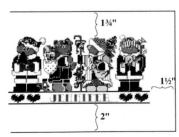

Figure 1

of design fabric. Using design fabric as pattern, cut white fabric (backing).

2. Fuse interfacing to back of design fabric, following manufacturer's instructions. With right sides facing, sew short edges of design unit together; trim seam and turn.

3. With right sides facing, sew short edges of backing together; trim seams.

4. Cut and piece 2"x20" and 1½"x5" bias strips from pindot fabric. Cut 20" of cotton cord. Using longer strip and cord, make piping; trim seam allowance to ½". With raw edges even, baste piping around right side of design unit along bottom edge, overlapping ends at seam.

5. With right sides facing, sew design unit and backing together along bottom edge; trim seam and turn.

6. Using graph paper, enlarge Stocking Pattern B (p. 106) and trace heel and toe patterns (p. 21). Using pattern B, cut 2 each from green print and plain green fabric. Using heel and toe patterns, cut one each from pindot fabric.

7. Cut 1"x6½" (A) and 1"x6" (B) bias strips from remaining white fabric. With right sides facing and using ¼" seam allowance, sew A strip to inside edge of heel piece; press strip away from heel. Fold strip

to back of heel and press. Repeat with B strip and toe piece.

8. With right side up, baste heel and toe pieces to top of one green print piece (stocking front; with toe pointing left) along raw edges. Sew heel and toe pieces to stocking front along seams between pin-dot fabric and bias strip (Fig. 2).

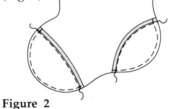

Figure 2

9. With right sides facing, sew stocking front and remaining green print piece together along sides and foot. Clip curves and turn right side out.

10. Sew plain green (lining) pieces together along sides and foot; leave 5" opening along one side. Trim seam allowance; clip curves.

11. For hanger, fold 5" bias strip in half lengthwise; sew long edge. Trim seam to ¼", turn, and press.

12. Fold hanger in half; sew to right side of lining back adjacent to back seam (with raw edges even).

13. With wrong side of cuff facing right side of print fabric and aligning seam of cuff with back seam of stocking unit, baste cuff to stocking unit around top edge.

14. Insert stocking unit into lining, right sides facing; sew together around top edge. Trim seam and turn. Slip-stitch opening in lining closed.▲

COLLECTOR'S CABINET

MATERIALS

- 7"-sq. White Aida 18
- Floss for motif (see key)
- Wooden mini collector's cabinet with 3¾"-sq.x1"-D design area
- 3⅝"-sq. **each** heavy cardboard and polyester fleece
- ¼ yd. green print fabric
- ½ yd. of ¹⁄₁₆"-dia. cotton cord
- 3¾"-sq.x½"-D plastic foam
- Tacky glue

INSTRUCTIONS

1. Using 2 strands of floss for cross-stitch, center and stitch two center bears and bottom border from *Teddy Bear Santas* on Aida.

2. Trim design fabric to 5" square, centering design.

3. Lightly glue fleece to cardboard (do not use cardboard included with cabinet).

4. Center fleece unit over back of design; pull fabric edges to back of cardboard and glue.

5. Cut and piece 1"x18" bias strip of green fabric. Using strip and cord, make piping; trim seam allowance to ½".

6. Glue flat edge of piping around back edge of design unit, overlapping ends at center bottom.

7. Insert plastic foam into design area and glue.

8. Insert design unit.♠

ORNAMENT

MATERIALS FOR ONE

- 6"x7" White Jobelan (28-ct.)
- Floss for motif (see key)
- ¼ yd. green print fabric
- ½ yd. of ³⁄₁₆"-dia. cotton cord
- Polyester fiberfill
- 5" **each** of ¹⁄₁₆"-W red and green satin ribbon
- Sewing thread

INSTRUCTIONS

USE ½" SEAM ALLOWANCE.

1. Using 3 strands of floss for cross-stitch, center and stitch one Santa bear from *Teddy Bear Santas* over 2 threads on Jobelan.

2. Trim design fabric ¾" beyond design on all sides. Using design fabric as pattern, cut print fabric (backing).

3. Measure circumference of design fabric. Cut and piece print fabric to make 1¼"-W bias strip 1"

longer than circumference of design fabric. Cut cord same length as strip. Using strip and cord, make piping.

4. With raw edges even, baste piping to right side of design fabric around edge; overlap ends at center top.

5. Fold green ribbon in half. Baste to center top edge of backing, raw edges matching.

6. With right sides facing, sew design and backing units together; leave 2" open along one side. Trim seams and turn.

7. Fill design unit with fiberfill. Slip-stitch opening.

8. Tie red ribbon into 1"-W bow. Tack to front of design unit at center top.♠

PLACE CARD

MATERIALS FOR ONE

- 4"-sq. white perforated paper (14-ct.)
- Floss for motif (see key)
- 3"x5" blank index card
- Repositionable tape
- Red chisel-point pen
- Small, sharp scissors

INSTRUCTIONS

1. Using 3 strands of floss for cross-stitch, center and stitch one heart from *Teddy Bear Santas*. Stitch one heart on each side of the center heart, leaving 6 squares between hearts.

Stitch green border line from *Teddy Bear Santas* across design paper, 2 squares below hearts.

2. Carefully cut around the upper half of the

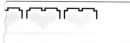

Figure 3

stitched hearts (Fig. 3).

3. Center and cut 1¾"x½" opening in design paper in area below border.

4. Cut index card ¼" bigger than opening. Center and write name on card. Tape card behind opening.

5. Fold design unit in half, wrong sides facing.♠

TABLE RUNNER

MATERIALS

- 15¾"x36½" White Jobelan (28-ct.)
- Floss listed in chart key; additional floss skeins needed— white(1), 321(2)
- ³⁄₈ yd. **each** red pindot and green print fabric
- Sewing thread

INSTRUCTIONS

1. Using 3 strands of floss for cross-stitch, stitch *Teddy Bear Santas* over 2 threads at each end of Jobelan, with bottom edge of design 1⅞" from fabric

edge; center side to side. Omit name and fill in border with hearts.

2. Trim 1" from all sides of design fabric.

3. Cut two 1¼"x34½" and two 1¼"x13¾" strips from red fabric. With right sides facing and using ⅝" seam allowance, sew long strips to long edges of design fabric, raw edges even. Press strips away from design unit. Repeat with short strips along short edges of design unit.

4. Cut two 2"x34½" and two 2"x14¾" strips from green fabric. With right sides facing and using ½" seam allowance, sew long strips to long edges of design unit, raw edges even. Press strips away from design unit.

5. Press remaining long edges under ½". Fold pressed edges to back of design unit and slip-stitch.

6. With right sides facing and using ½" seam allowance, sew short strips to short edges of design unit, long raw edges even and centered side to side. Press strips away from design.

7. Press ends of strips to back of design unit. Press remaining long edges under ½". Fold pressed edges to back of design unit and slip-stitch.♠

Continued on next page

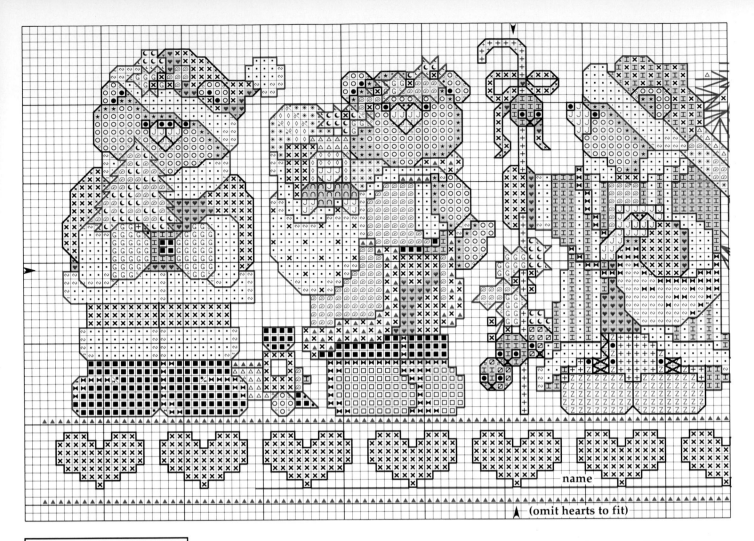

(omit hearts to fit)

PLACE MAT

MATERIALS FOR ONE

- 20¼"x14" White Jobelan (28-ct.)
- Floss for motif (see key)
- ⅜ yd. **each** red pindot and green print fabric
- Sewing thread

INSTRUCTIONS

1. Use 3 strands of floss for cross-stitch and stitch

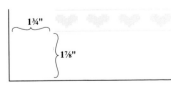

Figure 4

over 2 threads on Jobelan. Referring to Fig. 4 for placement, stitch border lines from *Teddy Bear Santas* across Jobelan; stop 1¾" from opposite end of fabric.

2. Beginning 4 threads from left end of border lines, center and stitch hearts between border lines, stopping 4 threads from right end.

3. Stitch one bear from *Teddy Bear Santas* in upper left corner, 1⅞" from edges. Trim 1" from all sides of design fabric.

4. Cut two 1¼"x12" and two 1¼"x18¼" strips of red fabric. With right sides facing and using ⅝" seam allowance, sew short strips to short edges of design

fabric, raw edges even. Press strips away from design unit. Repeat with long strips along long edges of design unit.

5. Cut two 2"x19¼" and two 2"x12" strips from green fabric. With right sides facing and using ½" seam allowance, sew short strips to short edges of design unit, raw edges even. Press strips away from design unit.

6. Press remaining long edges under ½". Fold pressed edges to back of design unit and slip-stitch.

7. With right sides facing and using ½" seam allowance, sew long strips to long edges of design unit, long raw edges even and centered side to side. Press

strips away from design.

8. Press ends of strips to back of design unit. Press remaining long edges under ½". Fold pressed edges to back of design unit and slip-stitch.♠

NAPKIN

MATERIALS FOR ONE

- 20¼"-sq. White Jobelan (28-ct.)
- Floss for motif (see key)
- ⅛ yd. **each** red pindot and green print fabric
- Sewing thread

INSTRUCTIONS

1. Use 3 strands of floss for cross-stitch and stitch over 2 threads on Jobelan.

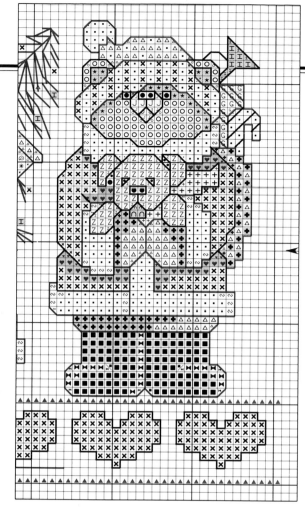

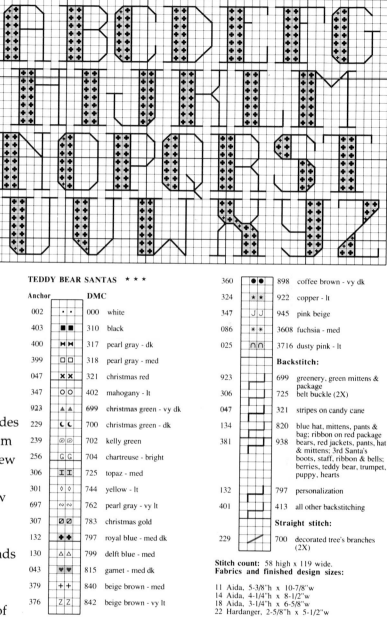

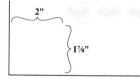

Figure 5

Referring to Fig. 5 for placement, stitch border lines from *Teddy Bear Santas* across Jobelan; stop 2" from opposite end of fabric.

2. Beginning 4 threads from left end of border lines, center and stitch hearts between border lines, stopping 4 threads from right end. Trim 1" from all sides of design fabric.

3. Press under long raw edges of design fabric ¼" twice. Topstitch edges.

4. Cut 1¼"x18¼" strip of red fabric. With right sides facing and using ⅝" seam allowance, center and sew strip to edge of design fabric below design, raw edges even. Press strip away from design unit. Press and baste short ends of red fabric to back of design unit.

5. Cut 2"x18¼" strip of green fabric. With right sides facing and using ½" seam allowance, center and sew strip to edge of design unit below design, raw edges even. Press strip away from design unit. Press ends of strip to back of design unit. Press remaining long edge under ½". Fold pressed edge to back of design unit and slip-stitch.✦

TEDDY BEAR SANTAS ★ ★ ★

Anchor		DMC	
002	· ·	000	white
403	■ ■	310	black
400	⋈ ⋈	317	pearl gray - dk
399	□ □	318	pearl gray - med
047	✕ ✕	321	christmas red
347	○ ○	402	mahogany - lt
923	▲ ▲	699	christmas green - vy dk
229	⊂ ⊂	700	christmas green - dk
239	⊘ ⊘	702	kelly green
256	G G	704	chartreuse - bright
306	I I	725	topaz - med
301	◇ ◇	744	yellow - lt
697	∾ ∾	762	pearl gray - vy lt
307	⊠ ⊠	783	christmas gold
132	✚ ✚	797	royal blue - med dk
130	△ △	799	delft blue - med
043	♥ ♥	815	garnet - med dk
379	+ +	840	beige brown - med
376	Z Z	842	beige brown - vy lt
360	● ●	898	coffee brown - vy dk
324	★ ★	922	copper - lt
347	J J	945	pink beige
086	＊ ＊	3608	fuchsia - med
025	∩ ∩	3716	dusty pink - lt

Backstitch:

923		699	greenery, green mittens & package
306		725	belt buckle (2X)
047		321	stripes on candy cane
134		820	blue hat, mittens, pants & bag; ribbon on red package
381		938	bears, red jackets, pants, hat & mittens; 3rd Santa's boots, staff, ribbon & bells; berries, teddy bear, trumpet, puppy, hearts
132		797	personalization
401		413	all other backstitching

Straight stitch:

229		700	decorated tree's branches (2X)

Stitch count: 58 high x 119 wide.
Fabrics and finished design sizes:

11 Aida, 5-3/8"h x 10-7/8"w
14 Aida, 4-1/4"h x 8-1/2"w
18 Aida, 3-1/4"h x 6-5/8"w
22 Hardanger, 2-5/8"h x 5-1/2"w

OLD-WORLD
SAINT NICHOLAS

Designed by Linda Gillum

It's hard to imagine a figure more

timeless than Saint Nicholas. And this magnificent

version, dressed in long robes and carrying a freshly

cut tree, captures all his traditional splendor. This

portrait is a dazzling centerpiece for stocking and ornament.

It's hard to imagine a figure more

timeless than Saint Nicholas. And this magnificent

version, dressed in long robes and carrying a freshly

cut tree, captures all his traditional splendor. This

portrait is a dazzling centerpiece for stocking and ornaments.

STOCKING

MATERIALS

- 15"x20" Cream Glasgow linen (28-ct.)
- Floss listed in chart key; additional floss skeins needed—white(3), 519(1), 747(1), 762(1)
- ½ yd. ivory moiré faille
- ½ yd. ivory cotton fabric
- 1¼ yds. of ⅜"-dia. metallic gold and beige twisted satin cord
- 4" of 1⁄16"-W red satin ribbon
- Tacky glue
- Sewing thread

INSTRUCTIONS

USE ½" SEAM ALLOWANCE.

1. Using 3 strands of floss for cross-stitch, center and stitch *Old-World Saint Nicholas* over 2 threads on linen. Center and stitch name on baseline.

2. Sew running stitches around outer edge of design (see chart), allowing an extra ⅛" beyond design at top edge. Trim fabric ½" beyond running stitches.

3. Using design fabric as pattern, cut one stocking back from faille and 2 lining pieces from cotton fabric.

4. With right sides together, sew stocking back to design fabric; leave top open. Clip curves and turn right side out.

5. Trim cord to fit sides and foot of stocking; glue ends to prevent fraying. Slip-stitch cord around sides and foot of stocking along seam.

6. For hanger, cut 1½"x5" bias strip from faille. Fold strip in half lengthwise; sew long edge. Trim seam to ¼", turn, and press.

7. Fold hanger in half; baste to right side of stocking back adjacent to cord (with raw edges even).

8. Sew lining pieces together along sides and foot, leaving 5" opening in one side. Trim seam allowance to ¼"; clip curves.

9. Insert stocking unit into lining, right sides facing; sew together around top edge. Trim seam and turn. Slip-stitch opening in lining closed.

10. Tie 1⁄16"-W ribbon into ½"-W bow; trim ends diagonally. Glue bow to raccoon's neck.

ORNAMENT

MATERIALS FOR ONE

- 5"x6" Cream Edinborough linen (36-ct.)
- Floss for motif (see key)
- 5"x6" **each** lightweight cardboard and ivory moiré faille
- 2⅝"x3⅝" oval Stik'N Puff
- 16" of ⅛"-dia. metallic gold and beige twisted satin cord
- 12" of 1"-W ivory satin premade pleated ruffle
- Tacky glue
- **For raccoon only**—4" of 1⁄16"-W red satin ribbon

INSTRUCTIONS

1. Using 2 strands of floss for cross-stitch, center and stitch raccoon, lantern, **or** wreath motif from *Old-World Saint Nicholas* over 2 threads on linen.

2. Trace Stik'N Puff onto back of design fabric (design centered), faille (backing), and cardboard. Trim fabrics 1" beyond traced line. Cut cardboard along line.

3. Center foam side of Stik'N Puff over back of design; remove backing paper. Press Stik'N Puff firmly against fabric. Pull fabric edges onto adhesive backing. Glue where edges overlap.

4. Center cardboard over backing fabric, pull edges to back, and glue.

5. Starting at bottom, glue ruffle around back edge of design unit, overlapping ends.

6. Cut cord to fit circumference of design unit; glue ends to prevent fraying. Beginning at center top, glue cord around design unit.

Continued on page 100

name

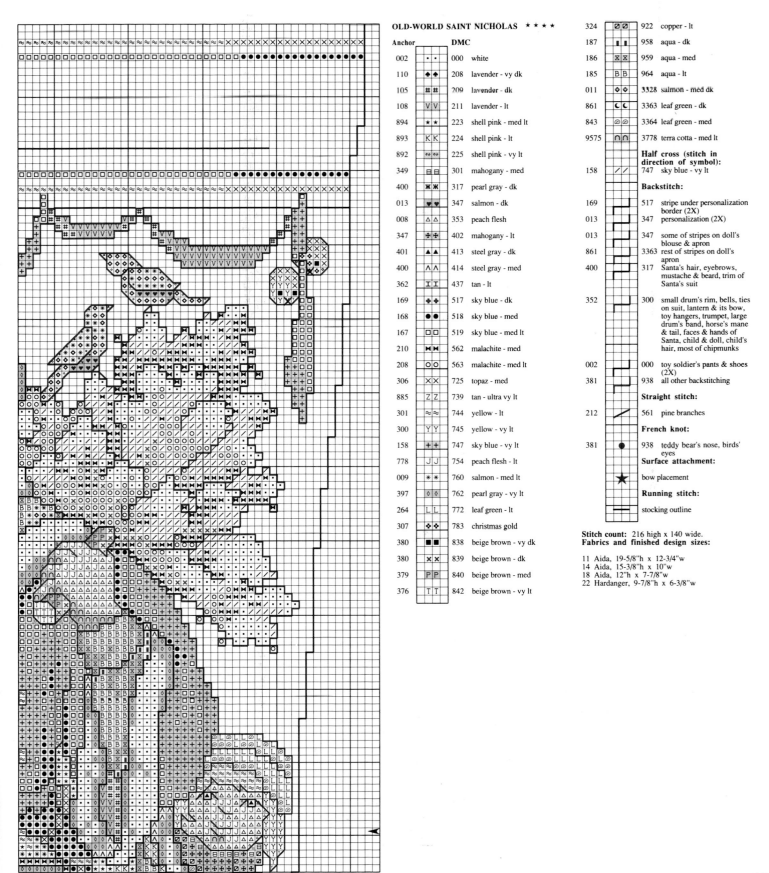

OLD-WORLD SAINT NICHOLAS ★ ★ ★ ★

Anchor		DMC	
002	· ·	000	white
110	◆ ◆	208	lavender - vy dk
105	✥ ✥	209	lavender - dk
108	V V	211	lavender - lt
894	★ ★	223	shell pink - med lt
893	K K	224	shell pink - lt
892	↔ ↔	225	shell pink - vy lt
349	⊟ ⊟	301	mahogany - med
400	✳ ✳	317	pearl gray - dk
013	♥ ♥	347	salmon - dk
008	△ △	353	peach flesh
347	✚ ✚	402	mahogany - lt
401	▲ ▲	413	steel gray - dk
400	∧ ∧	414	steel gray - med
362	I I	437	tan - lt
169	✦ ✦	517	sky blue - dk
168	● ●	518	sky blue - med
167	▫ ▫	519	sky blue - med lt
210	⋈ ⋈	562	malachite - med
208	O O	563	malachite - med lt
306	✕ ✕	725	topaz - med
885	Z Z	739	tan - ultra vy lt
301	≈ ≈	744	yellow - lt
300	Y Y	745	yellow - vy lt
158	+ +	747	sky blue - vy lt
778	J J	754	peach flesh - lt
009	✳ ✳	760	salmon - med lt
397	◊ ◊	762	pearl gray - vy lt
264	L L	772	leaf green - lt
307	❖ ❖	783	christmas gold
380	■ ■	838	beige brown - vy dk
380	✕ ✕	839	beige brown - dk
379	P P	840	beige brown - med
376	T T	842	beige brown - vy lt

Anchor		DMC	
324	⊠ ⊠	922	copper - lt
187	I I	958	aqua - dk
186	⊠ ⊠	959	aqua - med
185	B B	964	aqua - lt
011	◇ ◇	3328	salmon - med dk
861	C C	3363	leaf green - dk
843	⊘ ⊘	3364	leaf green - med
9575	⋂ ⋂	3778	terra cotta - med lt

Half cross (stitch in direction of symbol):

158	╱ ╱	747	sky blue - vy lt

Backstitch:

169		517	stripe under personalization border (2X)
013		347	personalization (2X)
013		347	some of stripes on doll's blouse & apron
861		3363	rest of stripes on doll's apron
400		317	Santa's hair, eyebrows, mustache & beard, trim of Santa's suit
352		300	small drum's rim, bells, ties on suit, lantern & its bow, toy hangers, trumpet, large drum's band, horse's mane & tail, faces & hands of Santa, child & doll, child's hair, most of chipmunks
002		000	toy soldier's pants & shoes (2X)
381		938	all other backstitching

Straight stitch:

212		561	pine branches

French knot:

381	●	938	teddy bear's nose, birds' eyes

Surface attachment:

★		bow placement

Running stitch:

		stocking outline

Stitch count: 216 high x 140 wide.
Fabrics and finished design sizes:

11 Aida, 19-5/8"h x 12-3/4"w
14 Aida, 15-3/8"h x 10"w
18 Aida, 12"h x 7-7/8"w
22 Hardanger, 9-7/8"h x 6-3/8"w

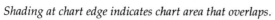

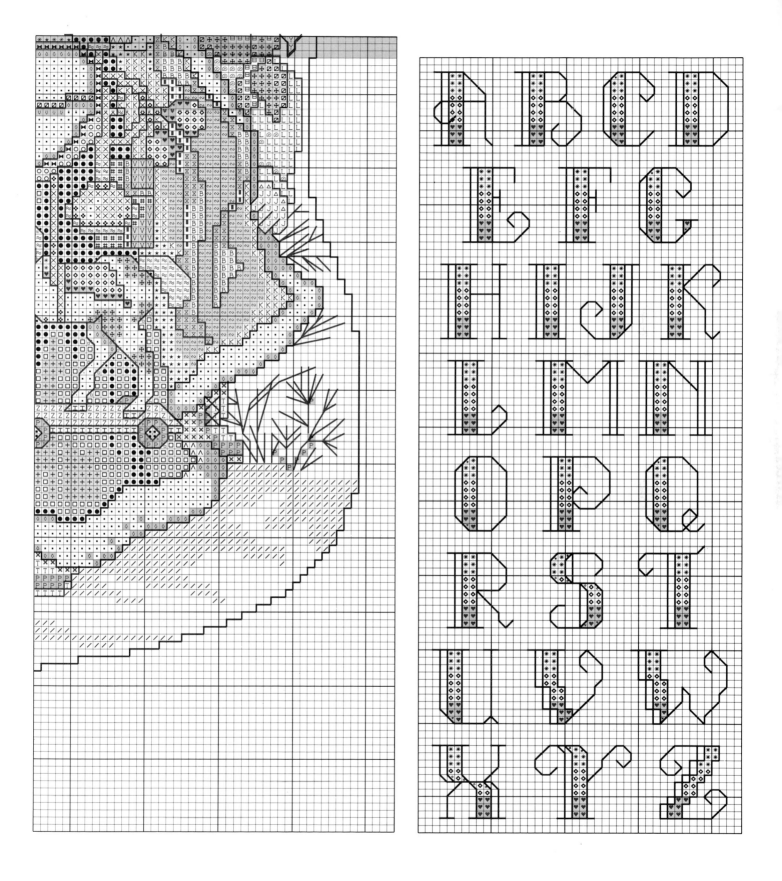

7. Fold remaining cord in half. Glue raw ends to back of design unit at center top.

8. Glue design and backing units together.

9. For raccoon ornament, tie ribbon into ½"-W bow; trim ends diagonally. Glue bow to raccoon's neck.▲

PILLOW

MATERIALS

- 12¼"x16" Cream Glasgow linen (28-ct.)
- Floss for motif (see key); additional floss skeins needed— white(3), 519(1), 762(1)
- 10¼"x14" lightweight fusible interfacing
- 1 yd. ivory satin fabric
- 1¼ yds. of ⅜"-dia. metallic gold and beige twisted satin cord
- ½ yd. of ⅝"-W ivory grosgrain ribbon
- Polyester fiberfill
- Sewing thread

INSTRUCTIONS

USE ½" SEAM ALLOWANCE.

1. Using DMC #347 and referring to *Glad Yul*, stitch saying vertically down left side of fabric; uppermost backstitching of G should be 2⅜" below top edge of fabric and left side of G should be 2¼" from left edge of fabric.

2. Stitch Santa from *Old-World Saint Nicholas*, aligning top of uppermost bird on tree with top of letter G. Right side of design should be 2¼" from right side of fabric.

3. Trim 1" from all sides of design fabric. Following manufacturer's instructions, fuse interfacing to back of design fabric.

4. Using design unit as pattern, cut satin (backing).

5. Cut and piece 7"x107" bias strip from remaining satin. With right sides facing, sew ends of strip together to form a loop. Fold loop in half length-wise, wrong sides facing; press. Sew gathering stitches ¼" and ½" from raw edges. Gather loop to fit outer edge of design unit. With raw edges even, baste loop around right side of design unit.

6. Sew design and backing units together, leaving 5" opening in one side; turn.

7. Fill design unit with fiberfill; slip-stitch opening closed.

8. Cut cord to fit seamline of design unit; glue ends to prevent fraying. Beginning in lower right corner, slip-stitch cord around seamline.

9. Tie ribbon into 4"-W bow; trim ends diagonally. Tack bow to lower right corner of pillow.▲

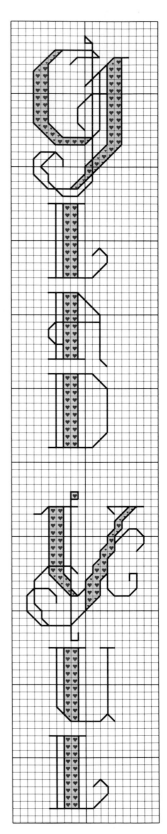

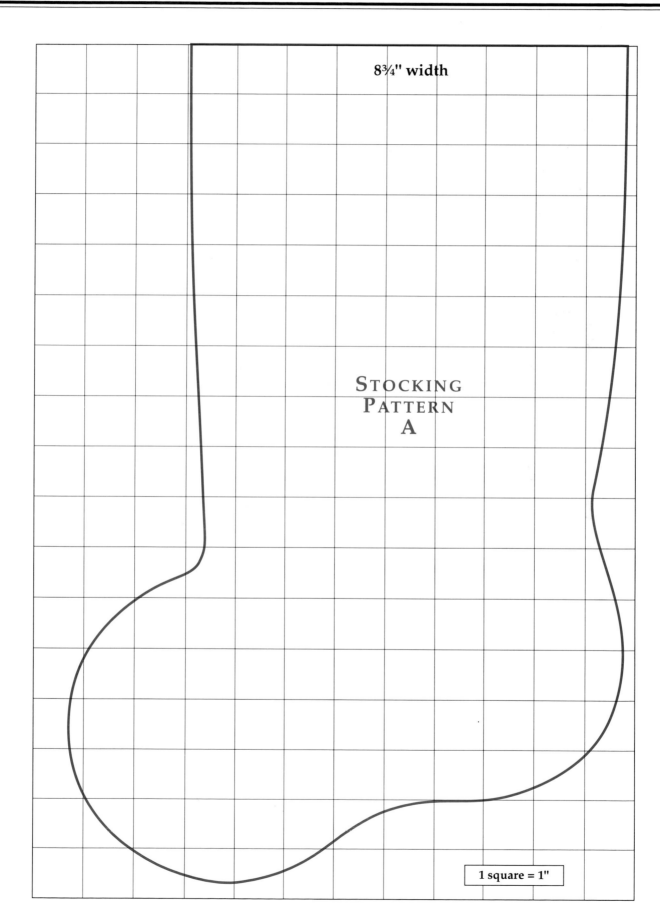

8¾" width

STOCKING
PATTERN
A

1 square = 1"

THE HERALD ANGELS

Designed by Nancy Rossi

With divine music, the angels in the heavens

rejoiced when Christ was born. As we celebrate this sacred event

each year, angels continue to represent the

hope and joy shared around the world during the holidays.

You can include angels in your

Christmas decorating by stitching this delicate design

on a stocking and table runner.

They'll be a beautiful reminder of all that there is to be

thankful for throughout this happy season.

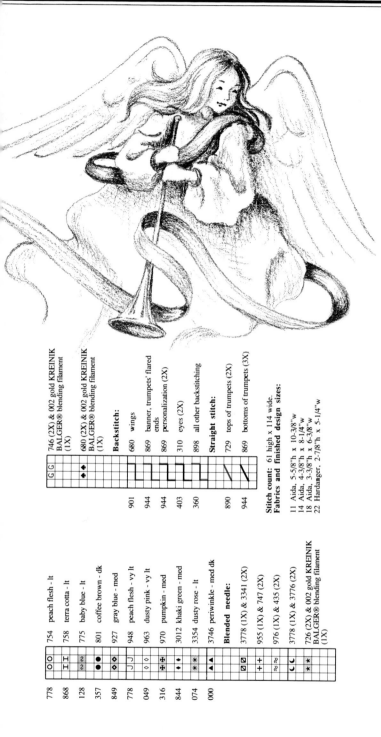

Chart Key

THE HERALD ANGELS ★★★

Anchor	DMC	Color
110	208	lavender - vy dk
104	210	lavender - med
894	223	shell pink - med lt
349	301	mahogany - med
403	310	black
047	321	christmas red
011	350	coral - med dk
351	400	mahogany - dk
371	433	brown - med
362	437	tan - lt
266	471	avocado green - lt
901	680	old gold - dk
295	726	topaz - lt
890	729	old gold - med
303	742	tangerine - lt
386	746	off white
778	754	peach flesh - lt
868	758	terra cotta - lt
128	775	baby blue - lt
357	801	coffee brown - dk
849	927	gray blue - med
778	948	peach flesh - vy lt
049	963	dusty pink - vy lt
316	970	pumpkin - med
844	3012	khaki green - med
074	3354	dusty rose - lt
000	3746	periwinkle - med dk

Blended needle:

- 3778 (1X) & 3341 (2X)
- 955 (1X) & 747 (2X)
- 976 (1X) & 435 (2X)
- 3778 (1X) & 3776 (2X)
- 726 (2X) & 002 gold KREINIK BALGER® blending filament (1X)

- 746 (2X) & 002 gold KREINIK BALGER® blending filament (1X)
- 680 (2X) & 002 gold KREINIK BALGER® blending filament (1X)

Backstitch:

Anchor	DMC	
901	680	wings
944	869	banner, trumpets' flared ends
944	869	personalization (2X)
403	310	eyes (2X)
360	898	all other backstitching

Straight stitch:

Anchor	DMC	
890	729	tops of trumpets (2X)
944	869	bottoms of trumpets (3X)

Stitch count: 61 high x 114 wide.
Fabrics and finished design sizes:

11 Aida, 5-5/8"h x 10-3/8"w
14 Aida, 4-3/8"h x 8-1/4"w
18 Aida, 3-3/8"h x 6-3/8"w
22 Hardanger, 2-7/8"h x 5-1/4"w

STOCKING

MATERIALS

- 19½"x8" Willow Green Aida 14
- Floss listed in chart key
- ¼ yd. light green fabric
- ½ yd. tan moiré faille
- ½ yd. tan cotton fabric
- ½ yd. of 1"-W ivory premade pleated satin ruffle
- ½ yd. of ³⁄₁₆"-W ivory braided gimp
- 1 yd. of ³⁄₁₆"-dia. cotton cord
- Sewing thread
- Graph paper

INSTRUCTIONS

USE ½" SEAM ALLOWANCE.

1. Referring to Fig. 1, stitch *The Herald Angels* on Aida, using 3 strands of floss for cross-stitch and centering name on baseline. Trim 1" from all sides of design fabric. Using design fabric as pattern, cut green fabric (backing).

2. With right sides facing, sew short edges of design fabric together; trim seam and turn.

3. With right sides facing, sew short edges of backing together; trim seams.

4. With right sides facing, sew design fabric to backing along bottom; trim seam and turn.

5. Position pleated edge of ruffle atop design unit, 2 squares below design and overlapping ends at center back with top end turned under ½"; baste.

6. Beginning at center back, topstitch gimp atop ruffle, 1 square below design.

7. Using graph paper, enlarge Stocking Pattern B (p. 106). Using pattern, cut 2 each from tan faille and cotton fabric.

8. Cut and piece remaining faille into 2"x36" and 1½"x5" bias strips. Using longer strip and cotton cord, make piping; trim seam allowance to ½".

Continued on page 107

Figure 1

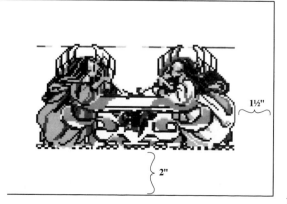

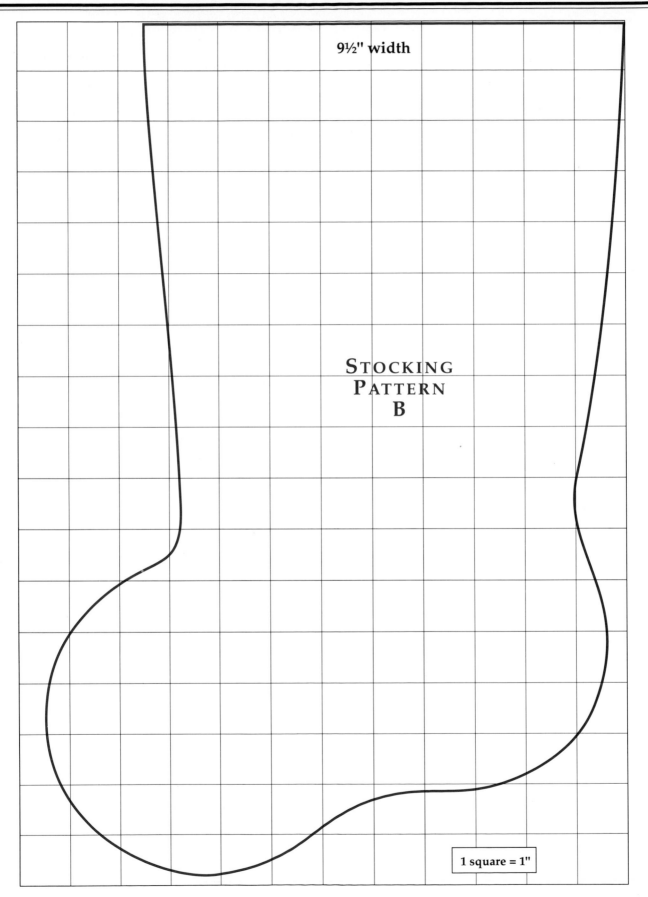

9½" width

STOCKING
PATTERN
B

1 square = 1"

9. With raw edges even and beginning 2" below top edge, baste piping to right side of one faille piece, along sides and foot, ending approx. 2" from top edge (Fig. 2).

Figure 2

10. With right sides facing, sew faille pieces together along sides and foot. Clip curves and turn right side out.

11. Sew tan cotton (lining) pieces together along sides and foot; leave 5" opening along one side. Trim seam allowance; clip curves.

12. For hanger, fold 5" bias strip in half lengthwise; sew long edge. Trim seam to ¼", turn, and press.

13. Fold hanger in half; sew to right side of lining back adjacent to back seam (with raw edges even).

14. With wrong side of cuff facing right side of faille and aligning seam of cuff with back seam of stocking, baste cuff to stocking around top edge.

15. Insert cuff unit into lining, right sides facing; sew together around top edge. Trim seam and turn. Slip-stitch opening in lining closed.♠

TABLE RUNNER

MATERIALS

- 15"x36" Willow Green Aida 14
- Floss listed in chart key; additional floss skeins needed— 746(1), 754(1), 963(1)
- ¾ yd. **each** 1"-W ivory premade pleated satin ruffle and ⅜"-W ivory braided gimp
- Sewing thread

INSTRUCTIONS

1. Using 3 strands of floss for cross-stitch, stitch *The Herald Angels* twice with bottom edge 1⅝" from short edges of Aida and centered side to side. Using alphabet, center and stitch "Rejoice" on baseline.

2. Trim ⅝" from each short edge of design fabric; zigzag-stitch.

3. Trim long edges of design fabric 2½" beyond design.

4. Press long edges under ¼". Turn another ¼" and topstitch.

5. Cut ruffle and gimp in half. Position pleated edge of one ruffle length atop design fabric, ⅜" above one short edge of design fabric and centered side to side; baste (Fig. 3). Topstitch one gimp length atop pleated edge of ruffle. Repeat with remaining lengths at opposite edge.

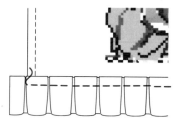

Figure 3

6. Turn ends of ruffle/gimp unit to back of design unit; tack in place.♠

Helpful Tips from Cross-Stitchers

When I'm stitching on Aida fabric, and the design has ¼ stitches, I keep a sharp straight pin handy, preferably one with a large, colored head. Before making the ¼ stitch, I pierce the center of the square with the straight pin. This makes stitching easier and assures that my ¼ stitches are centered in the square.
—*Edwina Cota*

After I pull out the floss colors for a project, I gather as many needles as I have colors. At the beginning of each new color, I thread a needle which stays with that color's floss skein until the project is completed. This way, whether the chart calls for one stitch or fifty, I'm ready to pick up the needle and sew.

—*Laura A. Neal*

When I get close to the end of a skein and discover that the next skein (of the same color) has a subtle dye-lot color difference, here's what I do to eliminate a noticeable change in a solidly stitched area. I save a length of the old skein, then blend it in with the new one. The ratio will vary: when working with three strands, first I'll use two old strands and one new one. Next, one old and two new. I finish up with three strands of the new skein. The color change is so gradual it's almost invisible.

—*Pam Ballast*

CHRISTMAS IN THE MANGER

Designed by Nancy Rossi

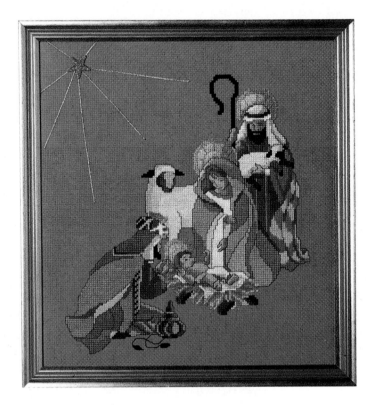

Celebrate the origin of Christmas with

this beautiful design. Mary and Joseph stand lovingly over the

newly born Christ child while a wise man kneels

in reverence and an angel rejoices in the heavens. Just as a

nativity scene is a part of Christmas decorating, this stocking,

framed piece, and ornament tell the story of how Christ

was born into this world. Enjoy this touching reminder

of the true meaning of Christmas.

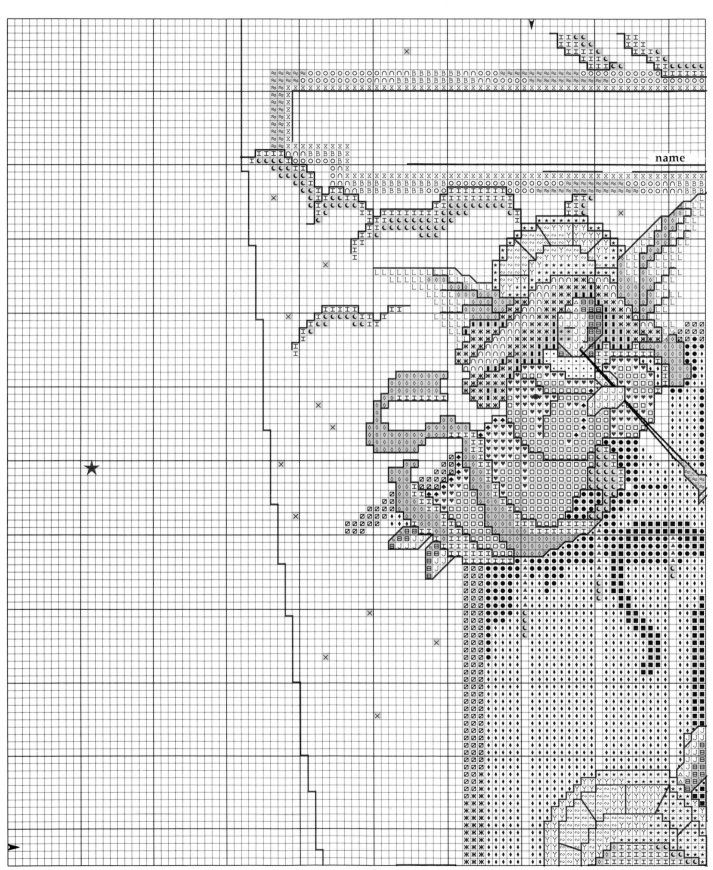

name

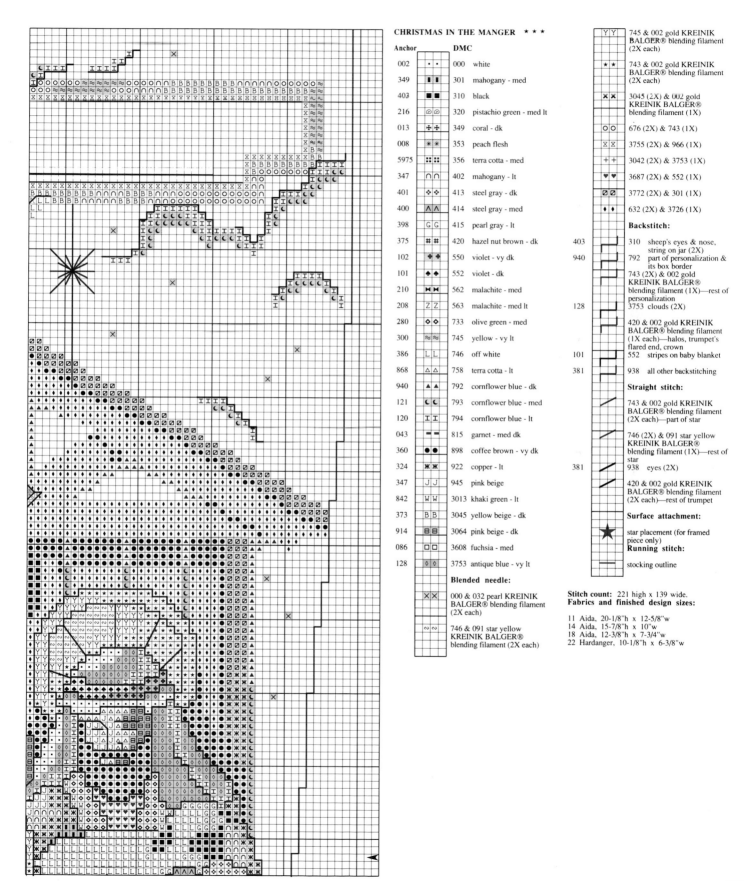

CHRISTMAS IN THE MANGER ★ ★ ★

Anchor		DMC	
002	• •	000	white
349	I I	301	mahogany - med
403	■ ■	310	black
216	⊘ ⊘	320	pistachio green - med lt
013	✚ ✚	349	coral - dk
008	✳ ✳	353	peach flesh
5975	⠶ ⠶	356	terra cotta - med
347	∩ ∩	402	mahogany - lt
401	❖ ❖	413	steel gray - dk
400	▲ ▲	414	steel gray - med
398	G G	415	pearl gray - lt
375	# #	420	hazel nut brown - dk
102	✦ ✦	550	violet - vy dk
101	◆ ◆	552	violet - dk
210	⋈ ⋈	562	malachite - med
208	Z Z	563	malachite - med lt
280	◇ ◇	733	olive green - med
300	≈ ≈	745	yellow - vy lt
386	L L	746	off white
868	△ △	758	terra cotta - lt
940	▲ ▲	792	cornflower blue - dk
121	C C	793	cornflower blue - med
120	I I	794	cornflower blue - lt
043	⚌ ⚌	815	garnet - med dk
360	● ●	898	coffee brown - vy dk
324	✹ ✹	922	copper - lt
347	J J	945	pink beige
842	W W	3013	khaki green - lt
373	B B	3045	yellow beige - dk
914	⊞ ⊞	3064	pink beige - dk
086	▫ ▫	3608	fuchsia - med
128	◊ ◊	3753	antique blue - vy lt

Blended needle:

✕ ✕		000 & 032 pearl KREINIK BALGER® blending filament (2X each)
∾ ∾		746 & 091 star yellow KREINIK BALGER® blending filament (2X each)

Y Y		745 & 002 gold KREINIK BALGER® blending filament (2X each)
★ ★		743 & 002 gold KREINIK BALGER® blending filament (2X each)
✕ ✕		3045 (2X) & 002 gold KREINIK BALGER® blending filament (1X)
O O		676 (2X) & 743 (1X)
X X		3755 (2X) & 966 (1X)
+ +		3042 (2X) & 3753 (1X)
♥ ♥		3687 (2X) & 552 (1X)
⊘ ⊘		3772 (2X) & 301 (1X)
◆ ◆		632 (2X) & 3726 (1X)

Backstitch:

403		310 sheep's eyes & nose, string on jar (2X)
940		792 part of personalization & its box border
		743 (2X) & 002 gold KREINIK BALGER® blending filament (1X)—rest of personalization
128		3753 clouds (2X)
		420 & 002 gold KREINIK BALGER® blending filament (1X each)—halos, trumpet's flared end, crown
101		552 stripes on baby blanket
381		938 all other backstitching

Straight stitch:

		743 & 002 gold KREINIK BALGER® blending filament (2X each)—part of star
		746 (2X) & 091 star yellow KREINIK BALGER® blending filament (1X)—rest of star
381		938 eyes (2X)
		420 & 002 gold KREINIK BALGER® blending filament (2X each)—rest of trumpet

Surface attachment:

★ star placement (for framed piece only)

Running stitch:

— stocking outline

Stitch count: 221 high x 139 wide.
Fabrics and finished design sizes:

11 Aida, 20-1/8"h x 12-5/8"w
14 Aida, 15-7/8"h x 10"w
18 Aida, 12-3/8"h x 7-3/4"w
22 Hardanger, 10-1/8"h x 6-3/8"w

Shading at chart edge indicates chart area that overlaps.

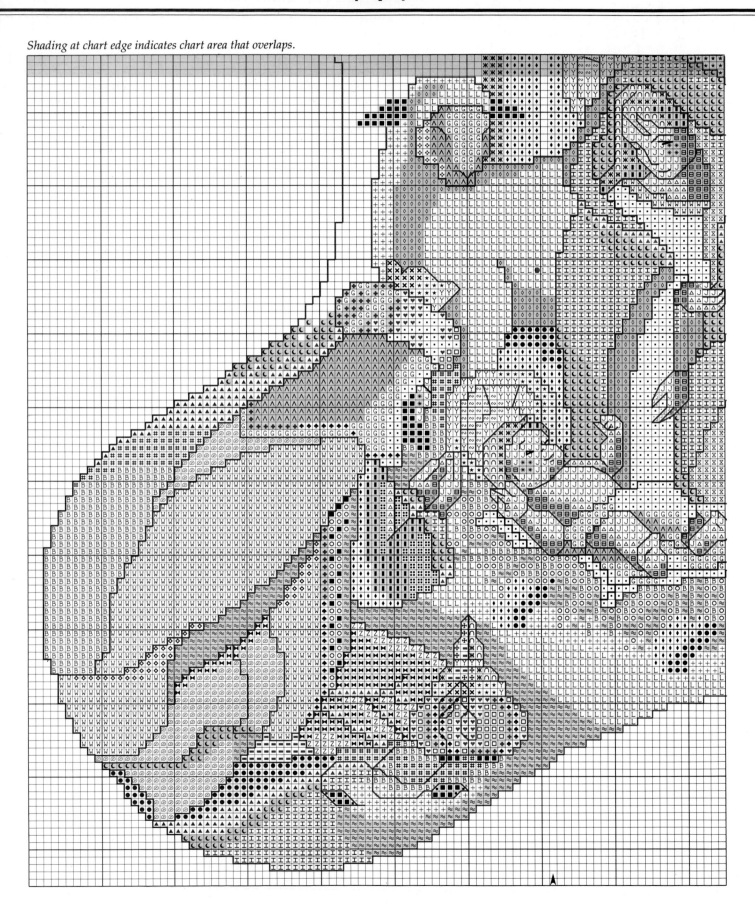

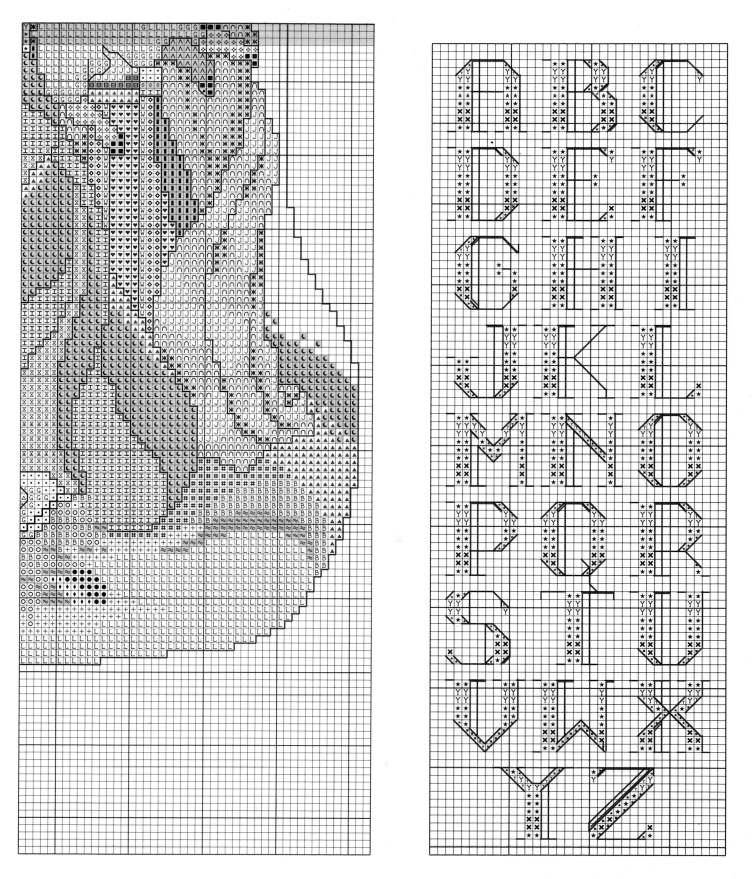

STOCKING

MATERIALS

- 15"x20" Colonial Blue Aida 14
- Floss listed in chart key; additional floss skeins needed—632(1), 746(1), 793(1), 794(1)
- ½ yd. light blue moiré faille
- ½ yd. light blue cotton fabric
- ¼ yd. gold lamé
- 1⅛ yds. of ³⁄₁₆"-dia. cotton cord
- Sewing thread

INSTRUCTIONS

USE ½" SEAM ALLOWANCE.

1. Using 3 strands of floss for cross-stitch, center and stitch *Christmas in the Manger* on Aida. Center and stitch name on baseline.

2. Sew running stitches around outer edge of design (see chart), allowing an extra ⅛" beyond design at top edge. Trim fabric ½" beyond running stitches.

3. Using design fabric as pattern, cut one stocking back from faille and 2 lining pieces from cotton.

4. Cut and piece lamé into 2"x40½" bias strip. Using strip and cord, make piping; trim seam allowance to ½".

5. With raw edges even, baste piping to right side of design fabric along sides and foot.

6. With right sides facing, sew stocking back to design unit; leave top open. Clip curves and turn right side out.

7. For hanger, cut 1½"x5" bias strip from remaining faille. Fold strip in half lengthwise; sew long edge. Trim seam to ¼", turn, and press.

8. Fold hanger in half; sew to right side of stocking back adjacent to piping (with raw edges even).

9. Sew lining pieces together along sides and foot, leaving 5" opening in one side. Trim seam allowance to ¼"; clip curves.

10. Insert stocking unit into lining, right sides facing; sew together around top edge. Trim seam and turn. Slip-stitch opening in lining closed.▲

ORNAMENT

MATERIALS

- 7"x8" Colonial Blue Aida 14
- Floss for motif (see key)
- 7"-sq. **each** gold fabric, polyester fleece, heavy and lightweight cardboard
- ½ yd. of ³⁄₁₆"-dia. metallic gold braided cord
- ⅝ yd. of ¼"-W metallic gold ribbon
- Three ½"-H gold-tone bells
- Tracing paper
- Tacky glue

INSTRUCTIONS

1. Using 3 strands of floss for cross-stitch, center and stitch angel motif from *Christmas in the Manger* on Aida, referring to blue dot for center.

2. Trace pattern; cut out. Trace pattern onto back of design fabric (design centered), gold fabric (backing), fleece, and cardboards. Cut fabrics 1" beyond traced line. Cut fleece and cardboards along line.

3. Glue fleece to heavy cardboard. Center design fabric right side up over fleece; pull edges to back and glue.

4. Center lightweight cardboard over backing fabric, pull edges to back, and glue.

5. Cut two 2½" and one 3" length of ribbon. Tie one bell to one end of each ribbon length. With longer ribbon positioned in center, glue remaining ends of ribbons to back of design unit, ½" above bottom point.

How to Master Fractional Stitches

1. Fractional stitches are used to smooth corners and curve lines. The three fractional stitches are ¼, ½, and ¾ (Fig. 1). The ¾ stitch is a combination ¼ and ½ stitch of the same color. Because it allows the fabric to show, the ½ stitch sometimes stands alone for subtle shading. **Note:** ½ stitches are not necessarily stitched in the same direction as the top thread of a full cross-stitch. When used in ¾ stitches, they are stitched in the direction of the diagonal line in the square on the chart. **2.** To make an *external* ¾

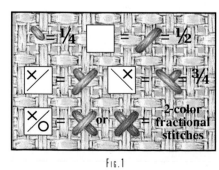

FIG.1

stitch (along the edge of a design), always make the ¼ stitch first, then the ½ stitch. (This allows you to correctly position the ¼ stitch.) Begin by bringing your needle up through the corner of the square which is the outer point of the ¼ stitch; then, on Aida fabric, stab down into the center of the square. On linen weaves, insert needle into the center hole, between threads.

6. Cut 4" length of ribbon; fold in half. Glue raw ends to back of design unit at center top.

7. Glue design and backing units together.

8. Trim cord to fit outer edge of design unit; glue ends to prevent fraying. Beginning at center top, glue cord around edges of design unit.

9. Tie remaining ribbon into 1½"-W bow; trim ends diagonally. Glue bow to center top edge of design unit.▲

FRAMED PIECE

MATERIALS

- 15"x16" Colonial Blue Aida 14
- Floss for motif (see key)
- 12"x13⅛" colonial gold frame with blue trim
- 1"-W appliqué gold fabric star
- 1 reel **each** 002C metallic gold Kreinik Balger cord and #16 braid

INSTRUCTIONS

1. Using 3 strands of floss for cross-stitch, center and stitch Mary, Joseph, Jesus, sheep, and wise man from *Christmas in the Manger* on Aida; blue dot indicates center of motif.

2. Position frame atop design fabric with bottom of wise man's robe ½" above front inside bottom edge of frame; center side to side. Lightly trace around inside back edge of frame.

3. Tack star to upper left corner of design fabric, with top of star ⅞" below top running stitches and left side of star 1⅜" from left running stitches.

4. Using braid, make 7 rays out from star (see photo); referring to Fig. 1, couch in place with cord.▲

Figure 1

ORNAMENT PATTERN

Always finish one of these *external* ¾ stitches by making a ½ stitch in the direction of the diagonal line on the chart.
3. To make *internal* fractional stitches (two colors meeting in one square: a ¾ stitch and a ¼ stitch), first decide which color to use for the ¾ stitch. Decide which of the colors represents a motif that is in the foreground. Using this color for the ¾ stitch

will make the motif stand out, adding perspective to the overall design. The usual exceptions are small detail features (such as eyes, lips, fingers, etc.), which may actually be in the background, but should be completed with ¾ stitches to keep them from getting "lost." To complete internal fractional stitches, again make both ¼ stitches first (in the different colors) and complete

with the ½ stitch in the color.
4. When backstitching around fractional stitches, hold the ½ stitch aside with your thumbnail. As you make the backstitch, lay it along the *outside* edge of the ½

stitch, taking care not to pull the stitch too hard. This keeps the backstitch from lying on top of the ½ stitch and allowing color to "bleed" under it (Fig. 2).

FIG. 2   hold back

SONGS OF JOY

Designed by Nancy Rossi

Christmas is filled with special sentiments that are often best when shared with family and friends. What better way to send a seasonal greeting to someone than with your favorite holiday sayings? Elegantly stitched on a stocking, ornaments, cards, and a framed piece, these sayings evoke ageless emotions and memories that are sure to fill everyone with the Christmas spirit.

name

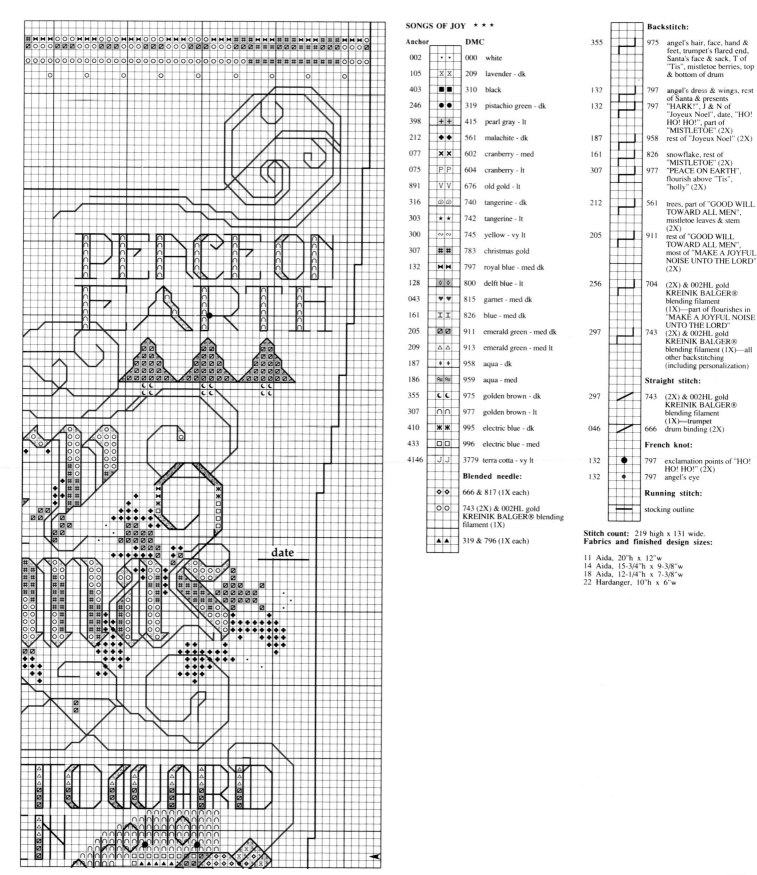

SONGS OF JOY ★ ★ ★

Anchor		DMC	
002	· ·	000	white
105	X X	209	lavender - dk
403	■ ■	310	black
246	● ●	319	pistachio green - dk
398	+ +	415	pearl gray - lt
212	◆ ◆	561	malachite - dk
077	X X	602	cranberry - med
075	P P	604	cranberry - lt
891	V V	676	old gold - lt
316	⊘ ⊘	740	tangerine - dk
303	★ ★	742	tangerine - lt
300	∽ ∽	745	yellow - vy lt
307	# #	783	christmas gold
132	◂▸ ◂▸	797	royal blue - med dk
128	◇ ◇	800	delft blue - lt
043	♥ ♥	815	garnet - med dk
161	I I	826	blue - med dk
205	⊠ ⊠	911	emerald green - med dk
209	△ △	913	emerald green - med lt
187	◆ ◆	958	aqua - dk
186	≈ ≈	959	aqua - med
355	C C	975	golden brown - dk
307	∩ ∩	977	golden brown - lt
410	⋇ ⋇	995	electric blue - dk
433	□ □	996	electric blue - med
4146	J J	3779	terra cotta - vy lt

Blended needle:

	◇ ◇	666 & 817 (1X each)	
	○ ○	743 (2X) & 002HL gold KREINIK BALGER® blending filament (1X)	
	▲ ▲	319 & 796 (1X each)	

Backstitch:

355		975	angel's hair, face, hand & feet, trumpet's flared end, Santa's face & sack, T of "Tis", mistletoe berries, top & bottom of drum
132		797	angel's dress & wings, rest of Santa & presents
132		797	"HARK!", J & N of "Joyeux Noel", date, "HO! HO!", part of "MISTLETOE" (2X)
187		958	rest of "Joyeux Noel" (2X)
161		826	snowflake, rest of "MISTLETOE" (2X)
307		977	"PEACE ON EARTH", flourish above "Tis", "holly" (2X)
212		561	trees, part of "GOOD WILL TOWARD ALL MEN", mistletoe leaves & stem (2X)
205		911	rest of "GOOD WILL TOWARD ALL MEN", most of "MAKE A JOYFUL NOISE UNTO THE LORD" (2X)
256		704	(2X) & 002HL gold KREINIK BALGER® blending filament (1X)—part of flourishes in "MAKE A JOYFUL NOISE UNTO THE LORD"
297		743	(2X) & 002HL gold KREINIK BALGER® blending filament (1X)—all other backstitching (including personalization)

Straight stitch:

297		743	(2X) & 002HL gold KREINIK BALGER® blending filament (1X)—trumpet
046		666	drum binding (2X)

French knot:

132	●	797	exclamation points of "HO! HO!" (2X)
132	·	797	angel's eye

Running stitch:

			stocking outline

Stitch count: 219 high x 131 wide.
Fabrics and finished design sizes:

11 Aida, 20"h x 12"w
14 Aida, 15-3/4"h x 9-3/8"w
18 Aida, 12-1/4"h x 7-3/8"w
22 Hardanger, 10"h x 6"w

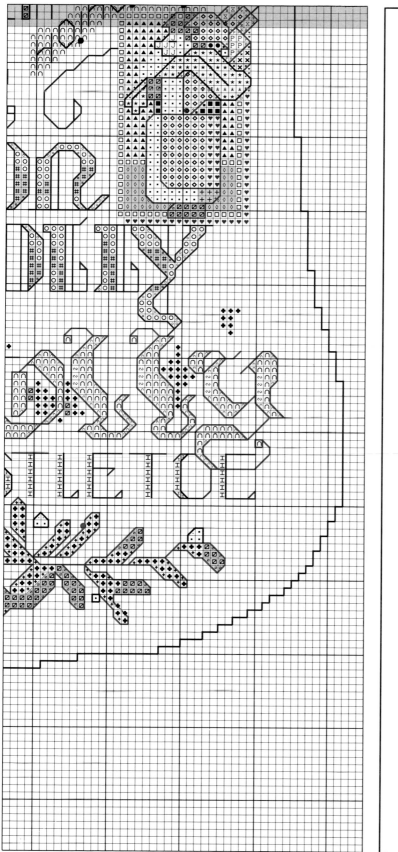

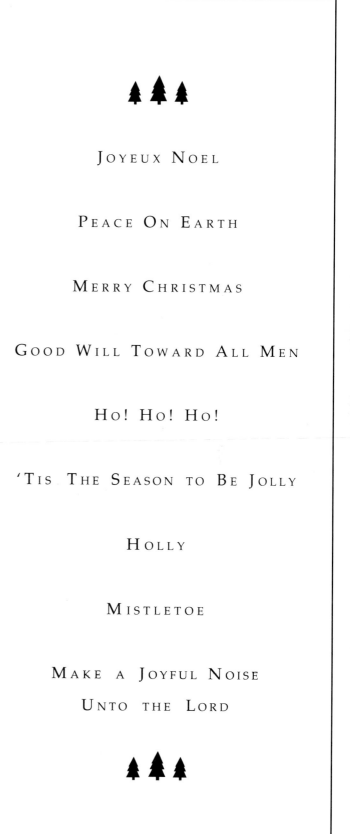

JOYEUX NOEL

PEACE ON EARTH

MERRY CHRISTMAS

GOOD WILL TOWARD ALL MEN

HO! HO! HO!

'TIS THE SEASON TO BE JOLLY

HOLLY

MISTLETOE

MAKE A JOYFUL NOISE
UNTO THE LORD

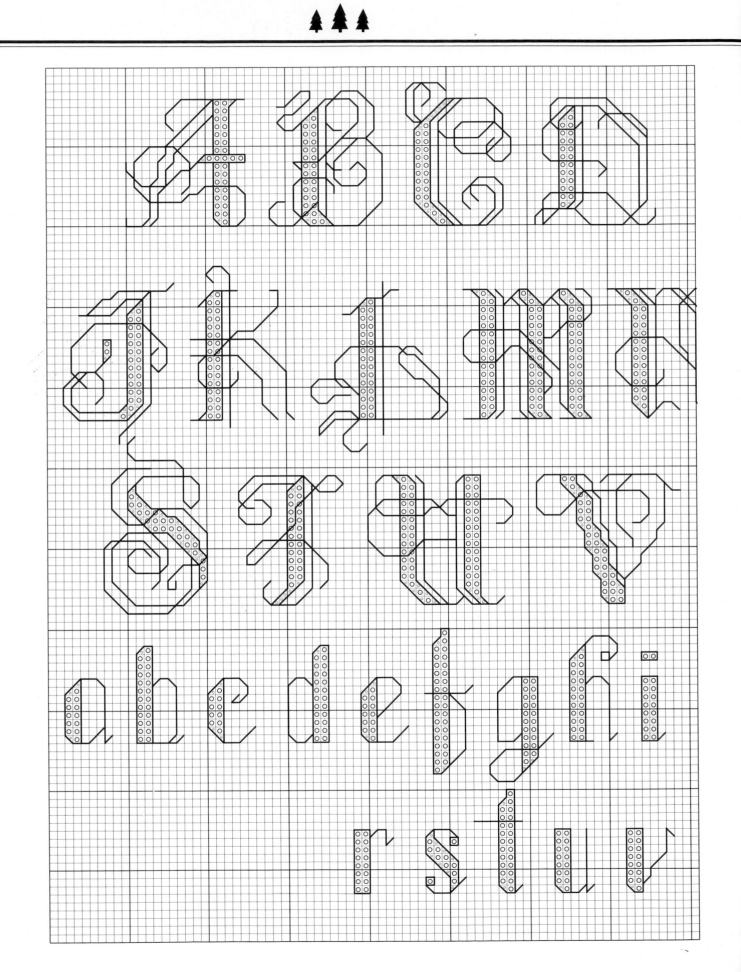

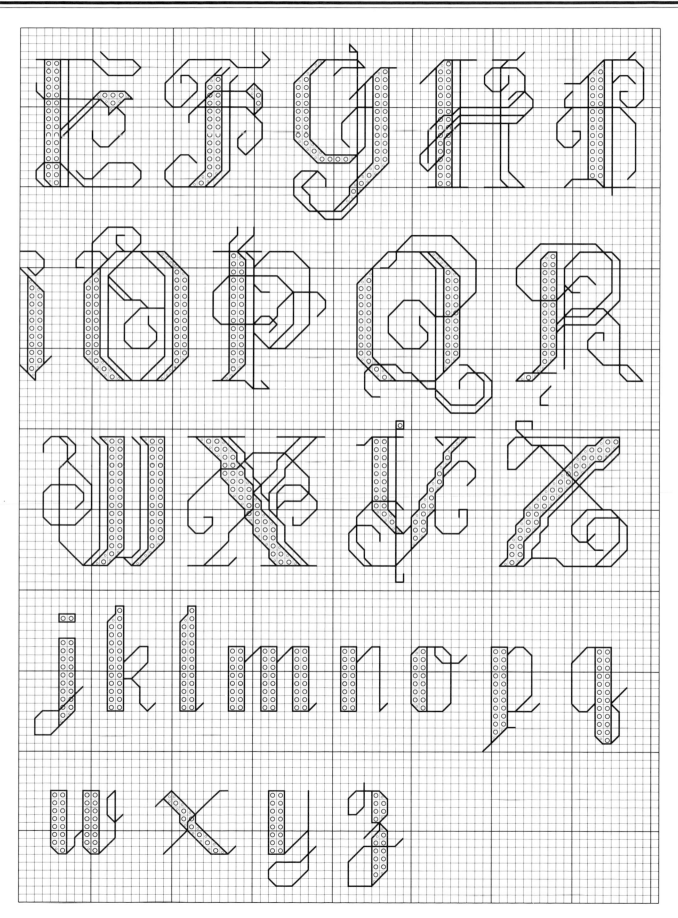

STOCKING

MATERIALS

- 15"x20" Red Aida 14
- Floss listed in chart key
- 1 yd. red fabric
- ¼ yd. green moiré taffeta
- 1¼ yds. of ³⁄₁₆"-dia. cotton cord
- Sewing thread

INSTRUCTIONS

USE ½" SEAM ALLOWANCE.

1. Center and stitch *Songs of Joy* on Aida using 3 strands of floss for cross-stitch. Center and stitch name on baseline.

2. Sew running stitches around outer edge of design (see chart). Trim fabric ½" beyond running stitches.

3. Using design fabric as pattern, cut one stocking back and 2 lining pieces from red fabric.

4. Cut and piece taffeta into 2"x40" bias strip. Using strip and cord, make piping; trim seam allowance to ½".

5. With raw edges even, baste piping to right side of design fabric along sides and foot.

6. With right sides facing, sew stocking back to design unit; leave top open. Clip curves and turn right side out.

7. For hanger, cut 1½"x5" bias strip from red fabric. Fold strip in half lengthwise; sew long edge. Trim seam to ¼", turn, and press.

8. Fold hanger in half; sew to right side of stocking back adjacent to piping (with raw edges even).

9. Sew lining pieces together along sides and foot, leaving 5" opening in one side. Trim seam allowance to ¼"; clip curves.

10. Insert stocking unit into lining, right sides facing; sew together around top edge. Trim seam and turn. Slip-stitch opening in lining closed.♠

ORNAMENT

MATERIALS FOR ONE

- Two 7"x6" pieces of Red Aida 14
- Floss for motif (see key)
- 4" of ⅛"-W red satin ribbon
- 6" of ⅛"-W green satin ribbon
- Polyester fiberfill
- Sewing thread

INSTRUCTIONS

1. Aligning blue dot on chart with center of design fabric, stitch "Mistletoe" or "Peace on Earth" motif from *Songs of Joy* (see photo) on one piece of Aida, using 3 strands of floss for cross-stitch.

2. Trim design fabric ⅞" beyond stitching on all sides. Using design fabric as pattern, cut remaining Aida (backing).

3. Fold red ribbon in half; baste raw ends to back of design fabric at center top, with ribbon ends ¾" below edge.

4. With wrong sides facing, topstitch design and backing fabrics together, ⅜" beyond design on all sides; leave 2" opening along bottom edge.

5. Fill design unit with fiberfill; topstitch opening closed.

6. Fringe fabric beyond stitching.

7. Tie green ribbon into 1"-W bow; trim ends diagonally. Tack bow to design unit at center top (see photo).♠

CARD

MATERIALS FOR ONE

- Red Aida 14 (6"-sq. for Santa or 8"x6" for angel)
- Floss for motif (see key)
- 8½"x11" piece of green card stock
- Tracing paper
- Tacky glue
- Sewing thread

INSTRUCTIONS

1. Aligning blue dot on chart with center of design fabric, stitch Santa or angel with "Joyeux Noel" motif from *Songs of Joy* on Aida, using 3 strands of floss for cross-stitch.

2. Trim design fabric ⅞" beyond design on all sides. Topstitch around design fabric, ⅜" beyond design on all sides. Fringe beyond topstitching.

3. Cut card pattern from tracing paper: 4½"x5⅛" for Santa or 6⅞"x5" for angel. Fold card stock in half to make 8½"x5½" rectangle. Aligning one long edge of pattern with fold, cut card stock.

4. Center and glue design unit atop one side of card stock.♣

FRAMED PIECE

MATERIALS

- 14"x11" Red Aida 14
- Floss for motif (see key)
- 10¾"x7½" gold-tone frame
- White mat with 7¾"x4½" opening
- 14"x11" green moiré taffeta
- Tacky glue

INSTRUCTIONS

1. Aligning blue dot on chart with center of design fabric, stitch "Merry Christmas" motif from *Songs of Joy* on Aida, using 3 strands of floss for cross-stitch.

2. To cover mat, lightly trace mat onto back of taffeta. Trim taffeta ¾" beyond traced lines on all sides (Fig. 1); clip inner

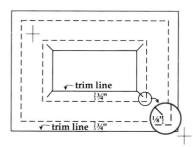

Figure 1

corners of rectangular opening to within ⅛" of traced lines.

3. Center taffeta right side up over mat, pull edges to back and glue.

4. Center and frame design with covered mat.♣

How to use Blending Filament

1. Unlike cotton floss, blending filament is slippery and slides out of the needle easily. To avoid this, tie the filament to the eye of the needle. For two strands of filament, cut a length twice as long as needed and fold it in half; insert the loop through the eye of the needle. Pull the loop over the point of the needle (Fig. 1), then tighten the loop at the end of the eye (Fig. 2). Then add floss

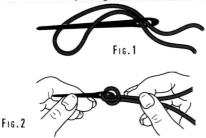

(if needed for blended needle). For four strands of filament, thread needle normally for the first two strands, then use method in Figs. 1 and 2 for the second two strands to secure all four strands to the needle.

For an uneven number of strands of filament, cut a length twice as long as needed; thread needle normally. Then cut a second length 2" longer than needed; tie to needle (Fig. 3); one end will be very short. When loop of second length is tightened it

will secure all strands to the needle. Add floss if required.

2. Stitch using 18" lengths. When stitching with a blended needle, strive to keep the filaments on top of the floss for maximum effect. Blending filament is not as flexible as floss; the challenge is to maintain even tension of all threads. If filaments separate from floss on a blended needle, stroke the fibers together, moving from design fabric to cut ends of fibers.

3. Couching usually gives a bolder outline and a smoother curve than backstitching. Make a long stitch (Fig. 4) with a heavyweight thread such as cable or braid upon the fabric or cross-stitches. Tack

down with very small stitches at regular intervals with a second, lighter-weight thread in a separate needle. These tack stitches are usually done with one strand of floss or filament in a matching or contrasting color.

Specialty threads are hand washable and dry-cleanable. Do not iron directly onto or use steam with metallics.

ACKNOWLEDGMENTS

This book could only have come about through dedicated teamwork and the assistance of many talented individuals who shared their time, effort, expertise, and products. We would like to express our appreciation and gratitude to the many people and companies who helped us create it.

STITCHERS

For their remarkable efforts in turning charts, fabric, and floss into beautiful stitched designs, we thank these needlecrafters:

Karen Baker

Grace Bushman

Theresa Caselman

Vicki Chinn

Julie Collins

Kay Draisin

Diane Earnest

Frances Egbert

Marilyn Fennell

Laurie Grant

Hank Haiungs

Joy Hancock

Amyee Johnson

Nancy Kuelbs

Kathy Lyons

Susan McAndrew

Terry Modrow

Peggy Morrissey

Angela Narducci-Brown

Susanna Pratt

Ann Sanchez

Linda Scott

Debbie Smith

Sharon Sommers

Sandra Telljohann

Janis Traub

Tracy Turner

Denise Warren

Kathi Westfall

Nancy Withrow

PHOTOGRAPHERS

For showing the projects in the best possible light, we thank:

Jay Graham
See pages 16, 23, 30, 38, 39, 54–56, 70–73, 102, 109

Dianne Woods
See cover and pages 6, 7, 14, 15, 22, 31, 32, 36, 37, 46–48, 52, 53, 64–66, 84–87, 92–94, 103, 108, 116, 117

PHOTO STYLISTS

For all the added touches that complement the projects, we thank:

Ina Klickstein

Gail Marell

LOCATIONS

Thanks, too, to the following people and companies for allowing us to photograph the projects at their private residences or places of business:

J. Goldsmith Antiques,
San Francisco, CA

The Inn, San Francisco, CA

Miller & Associates,
Tahoe City, CA

Jerry Lynn Van Scoy,
San Anselmo, CA

MANUFACTURERS AND SUPPLIERS

For fibers, fabrics, frames, and all other materials and accessories used in *Christmas Stockings in Cross-Stitch*, our special thanks to the following:

Aleene's/Artis
85 Industrial Way
Buellton, CA 93427
For glue

Anne Brinkley Designs
21 Ransom Road
Newton Center, MA 02159
For pendant

Banar Designs
P.O. Box 483
Fallbrook, CA 92028
For Stik'N Puffs

Charles Craft
P.O. Box 1049
Laurinburg, NC 28353
For Light Blue Aida, Pink Aida, Red Aida, Black Aida, Willow Green Aida, Light Oatmeal Fiddler's Lite, Tea-dyed linen, Natural linen

C. M. Offray & Son
41 Madison Avenue,
Floor 12
New York, NY 10010
For ribbon

Designs by
Liz Turner Diehl, Inc.
2252 W. 29th Avenue
Eugene, OR 97405
For Needlework Finisher

DMC Corporation
Port Kearny Building #10
South Kearny, NJ 07032
For floss

Four Corners Framing
Products
1741 Masters Lane
Lexington, KY 40502
For frame on p. 30

Harborview Frames
1559 Harborview Road
Charlestown, SC 29412
For frame on p. 108

Hickory Mountain Frames
P.O. Box 278
Reidsville, NC 27323
For pegged dome frame

Janlynn Corp.
34 Front Street, Box 66
Indian Orchard, MA 01151
For bibs

continued on next page

Kreinik Mfg. Co. Inc.
P.O. Box 1966
Parkersburg, WV 26102
*For Kreinik Balger® blending
filament and other specialty
threads*

Norden Crafts
P.O. Box 1
Glenview, IL 60025
For bellpull hardware

Prym-Dritz
P.O. Box 5028
Spartanburg, NC 29304
For Craf-T-Fleece

Serendipity Designs
11301 International Drive
Richmond, VA 23236
*For mats on pp. 30 and 116;
frame on p. 116*

Sudberry House
Box 895
Old Lyme, CT 06371
For collector's cabinet

Sue Hillis Designs
Box 2263
Petersburg, VA 23804
For sweater

Tin Originals
P.O. Box 64037
Fayetteville, NC 28306
*For tin lamp, heart,
wreath holder*

Wheatland Crafts
Route 5, Scuffletown Road
Simpsonville, SC 29681
For oval frame on p. 23

Whimpole Street Creations
P.O. Box 395
West Bountiful, UT 84087
For Battenburg lace

Wichelt Imports
Rural Route 1
Stoddard, WI 54658
*For Forget-Me-Not Blue Aida,
Denim Blue Aida,
White Jobelan*

Yarn Tree Designs
P.O. Box 724
Ames, IA 50010
For perforated paper

Zweigart/Joan Toggitt Ltd.
Weston Canal Plaza
2 Riverview Drive
Somerset, NJ 08873
*For White Aida, Ivory Aida, Ivory
Jubilee, White Glasgow linen,
Cream Glasgow linen, Cream
Edinborough linen,
waste canvas*